# THESEUS
## BATTLING THE MINOTAUR

A
GREEK
MYTH

STORY BY
**JEFF LIMKE**
PENCILS AND INKS BY
**JOHN McCREA**

EUROPE

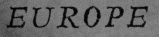

ITALY

MEDITERRANEAN SEA

# THESEUS

## BATTLING THE MINOTAUR

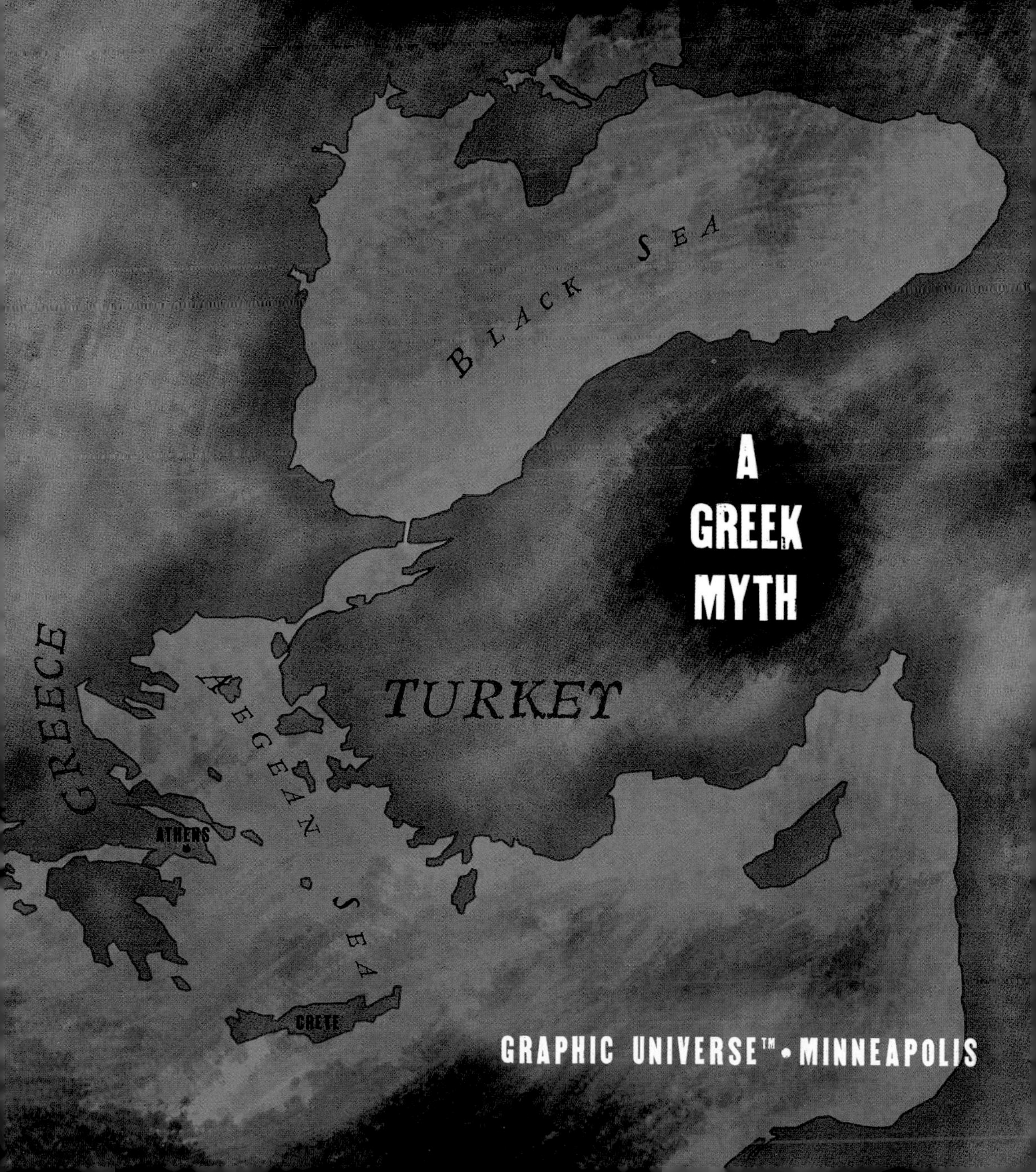
BLACK SEA
TURKEY
GREECE
AEGEAN SEA
ATHENS
CRETE

A GREEK MYTH

GRAPHIC UNIVERSE™ • MINNEAPOLIS

THESEUS IS ONE OF THE GREATEST HEROES OF GREEK MYTHOLOGY. HIS FEATS OF STRENGTH AND COURAGE HAVE BEEN PASSED DOWN FROM GENERATION TO GENERATION FOR MORE THAN 2000 YEARS. THIS PARTICULAR BOOK FOLLOWS THESEUS' EARLY ADVENTURES, AS HE COMES OF AGE AND ATTEMPTS TO FULFILL HIS DESTINY AS A GREAT HERO AND ATHENS' GREATEST KING. TO CRAFT THIS TALE FOR THE GRAPHIC MYTHS AND LEGENDS SERIES, AUTHOR JEFF LIMKE CONSULTED TWO OF THE MOST FAMOUS ANTHOLOGIES OF GREEK MYTHS, EDITH HAMILTON'S *MYTHOLOGY* AND *BULFINCH'S MYTHOLOGY* BY THOMAS BULFINCH. ARTIST JOHN McCREA REFERENCED NUMEROUS HISTORICAL AND TRADITIONAL SOURCES TO GIVE THE ART AN AUTHENTIC LOOK, FROM CLASSICAL GREEK ARCHITECTURE TO THE CLOTHING, WEAPONS, AND ARMOR WORN BY THE CHARACTERS. PROFESSOR DAVID MULROY ENSURED HISTORICAL AND VISUAL ACCURACY.

STORY BY JEFF LIMKE

PENCILS AND INKS BY JOHN McCREA

COLORING BY HI-FI COLOUR DESIGN

LETTERING BY HI-FI COLOUR DESIGN

CONSULTANT: DAVID MULROY, PH.D.
UNIVERSITY OF WISCONSIN-MILWAUKEE

Copyright © 2008 by Lerner Publishing Group, Inc.

Graphic Universe™ is a trademark of Lerner Publishing Group, Inc.

Graphic Universe™
A division of Lerner Publishing Group, Inc.
241 First Avenue North
Minneapolis, MN 55401 U.S.A.

Website address: www.lernerbooks.com

Library of Congress Cataloging-in-Publication Data

Limke, Jeff.
    Theseus : battling the Minotaur / by Jeff Limke ; illustrations by John McCrea.
        p.    cm. — (Graphic myths and legends)
    Includes index.
        ISBN 978-0-8225-6756-1 (lib. bdg. : alk. paper)
    1. Theseus (Greek mythology)—Juvenile literature.
    2. Minotaur (Greek mythology)—Juvenile literature.
    I. McCrea, John, artist/creator.  II. Title.
    BL820.T5L56    2008
    741.5'973—dc22                                          2007001829

Manufactured in the United States of America
2  3  4  5  6  7  -  DP  -  13  12  11  10  09  08

# TABLE OF CONTENTS

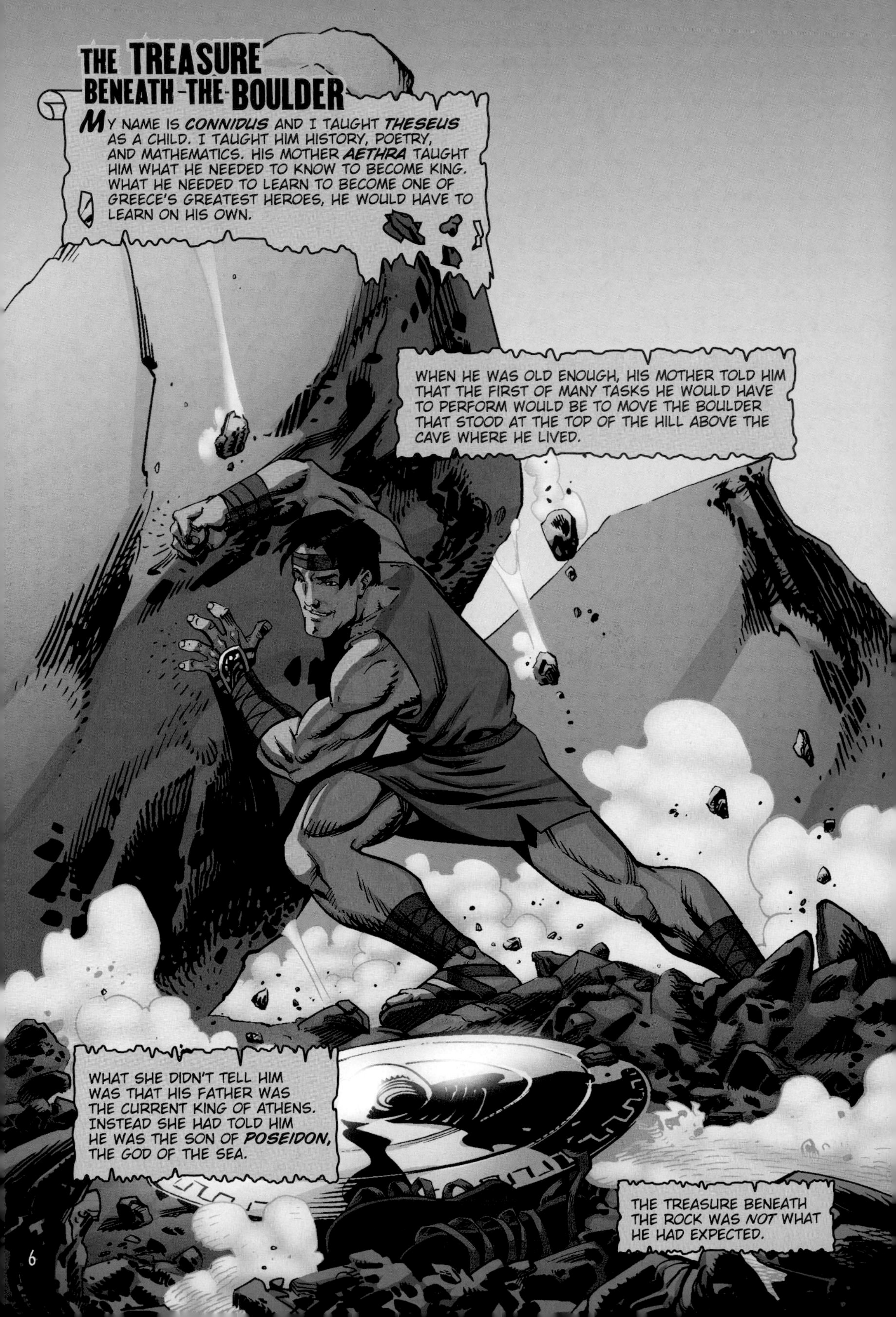

THE TREASURE BENEATH-THE-BOULDER
MY NAME IS *CONNIDUS* AND I TAUGHT *THESEUS* AS A CHILD. I TAUGHT HIM HISTORY, POETRY, AND MATHEMATICS. HIS MOTHER *AETHRA* TAUGHT HIM WHAT HE NEEDED TO KNOW TO BECOME KING. WHAT HE NEEDED TO LEARN TO BECOME ONE OF GREECE'S GREATEST HEROES, HE WOULD HAVE TO LEARN ON HIS OWN.
WHEN HE WAS OLD ENOUGH, HIS MOTHER TOLD HIM THAT THE FIRST OF MANY TASKS HE WOULD HAVE TO PERFORM WOULD BE TO MOVE THE BOULDER THAT STOOD AT THE TOP OF THE HILL ABOVE THE CAVE WHERE HE LIVED.
WHAT SHE DIDN'T TELL HIM WAS THAT HIS FATHER WAS THE CURRENT KING OF ATHENS. INSTEAD SHE HAD TOLD HIM HE WAS THE SON OF *POSEIDON*, THE GOD OF THE SEA.
THE TREASURE BENEATH THE ROCK WAS *NOT* WHAT HE HAD EXPECTED.

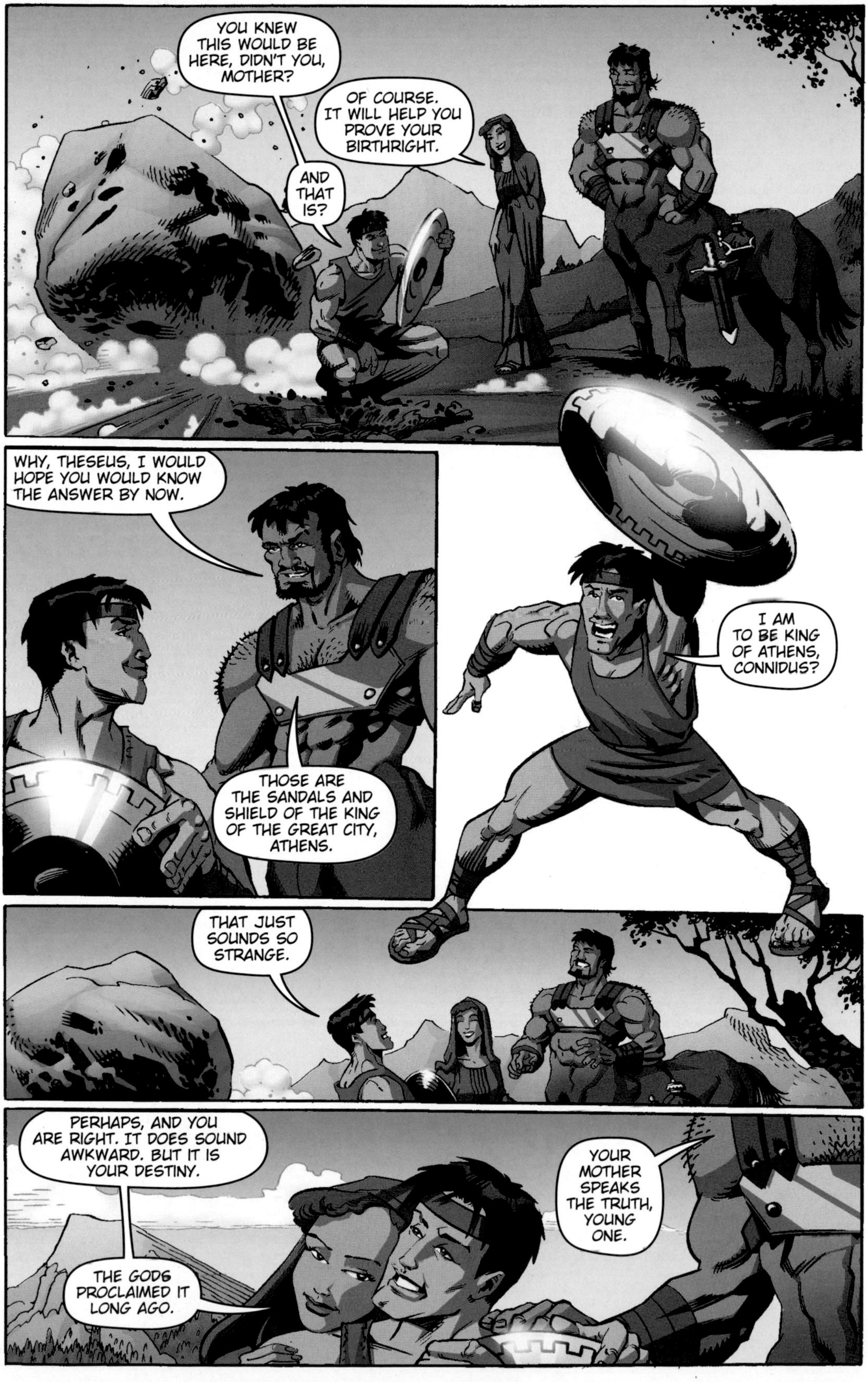
YOU KNEW THIS WOULD BE HERE, DIDN'T YOU, MOTHER?
OF COURSE. IT WILL HELP YOU PROVE YOUR BIRTHRIGHT.
AND THAT IS?
WHY, THESEUS, I WOULD HOPE YOU WOULD KNOW THE ANSWER BY NOW.
THOSE ARE THE SANDALS AND SHIELD OF THE KING OF THE GREAT CITY, ATHENS.
I AM TO BE KING OF ATHENS, CONNIDUS?
THAT JUST SOUNDS SO STRANGE.
PERHAPS, AND YOU ARE RIGHT. IT DOES SOUND AWKWARD. BUT IT IS YOUR DESTINY.
THE GODS PROCLAIMED IT LONG AGO.
YOUR MOTHER SPEAKS THE TRUTH, YOUNG ONE.

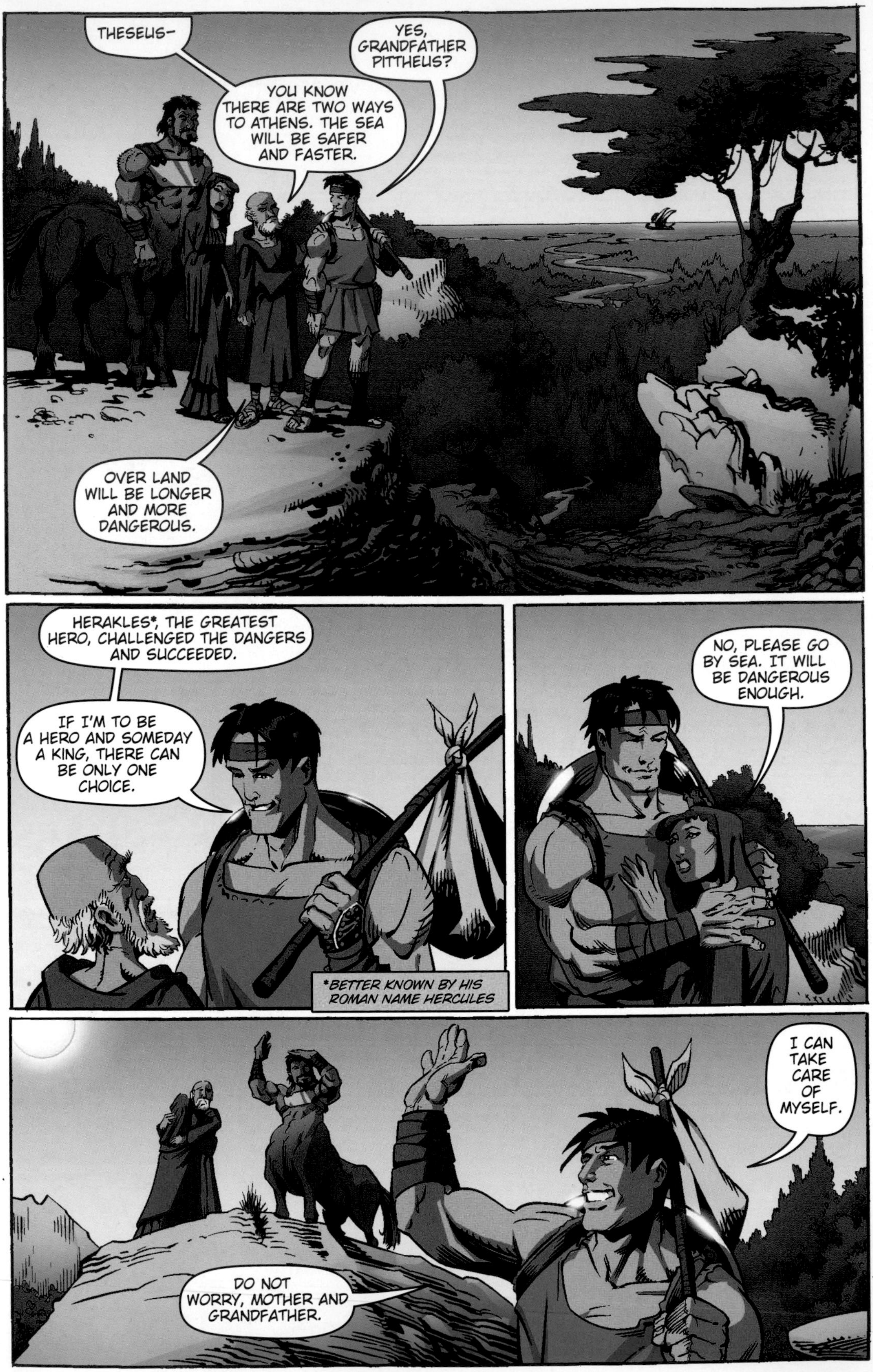
THESEUS–
YES, GRANDFATHER PITTHEUS?
YOU KNOW THERE ARE TWO WAYS TO ATHENS. THE SEA WILL BE SAFER AND FASTER.
OVER LAND WILL BE LONGER AND MORE DANGEROUS.
HERAKLES*, THE GREATEST HERO, CHALLENGED THE DANGERS AND SUCCEEDED.
IF I'M TO BE A HERO AND SOMEDAY A KING, THERE CAN BE ONLY ONE CHOICE.
*BETTER KNOWN BY HIS ROMAN NAME HERCULES
NO, PLEASE GO BY SEA. IT WILL BE DANGEROUS ENOUGH.
DO NOT WORRY, MOTHER AND GRANDFATHER.
I CAN TAKE CARE OF MYSELF.

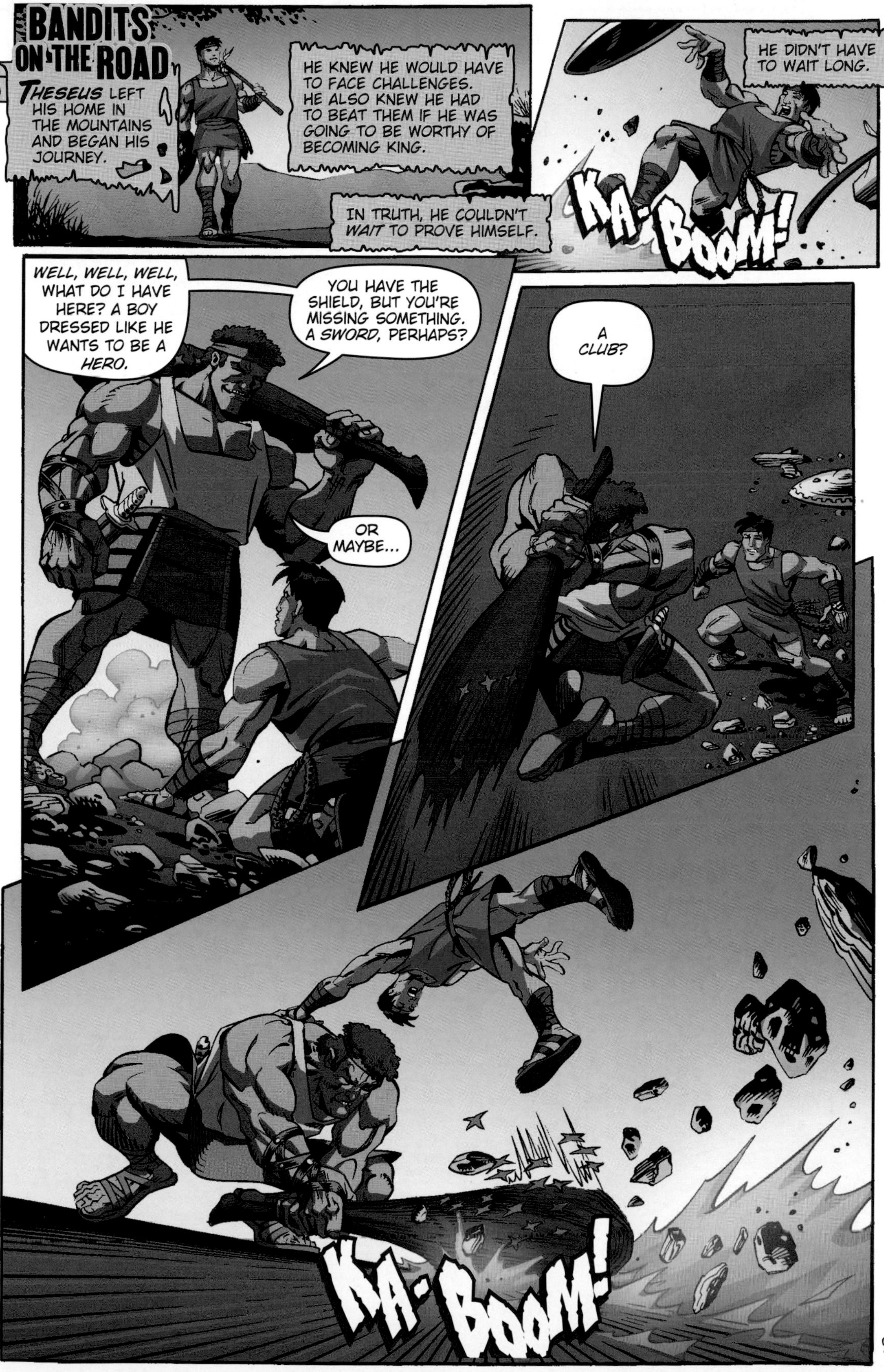
BANDITS ON THE ROAD
THESEUS LEFT HIS HOME IN THE MOUNTAINS AND BEGAN HIS JOURNEY.
HE KNEW HE WOULD HAVE TO FACE CHALLENGES. HE ALSO KNEW HE HAD TO BEAT THEM IF HE WAS GOING TO BE WORTHY OF BECOMING KING.
IN TRUTH, HE COULDN'T WAIT TO PROVE HIMSELF.
HE DIDN'T HAVE TO WAIT LONG.
KA-BOOM!
WELL, WELL, WELL, WHAT DO I HAVE HERE? A BOY DRESSED LIKE HE WANTS TO BE A HERO.
YOU HAVE THE SHIELD, BUT YOU'RE MISSING SOMETHING. A SWORD, PERHAPS?
OR MAYBE...
A CLUB?
KA-BOOM!

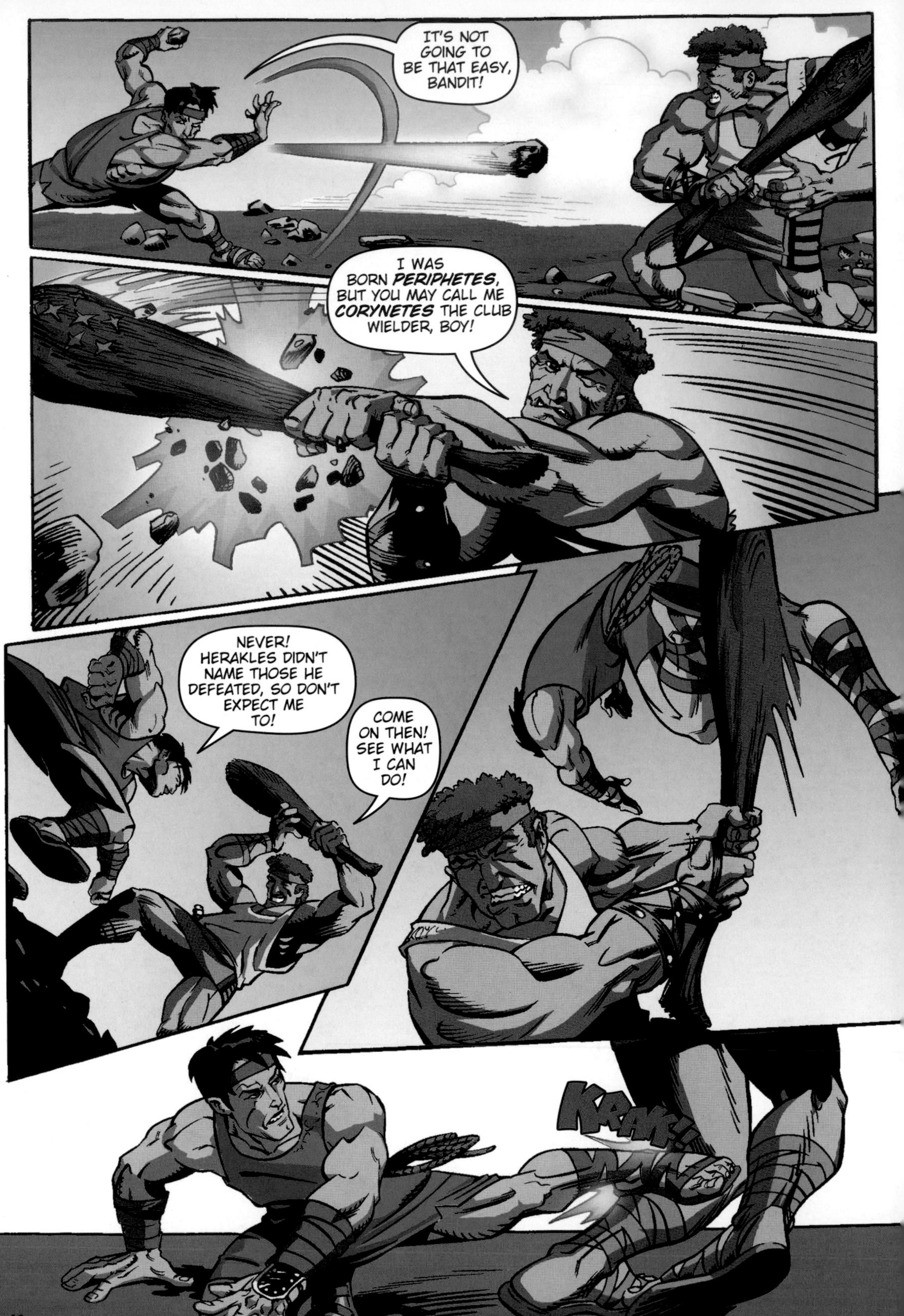

IT'S NOT GOING TO BE THAT EASY, BANDIT!
I WAS BORN PERIPHETES, BUT YOU MAY CALL ME CORYNETES THE CLUB WIELDER, BOY!
NEVER! HERAKLES DIDN'T NAME THOSE HE DEFEATED, SO DON'T EXPECT ME TO!
COME ON THEN! SEE WHAT I CAN DO!
KRAK!!

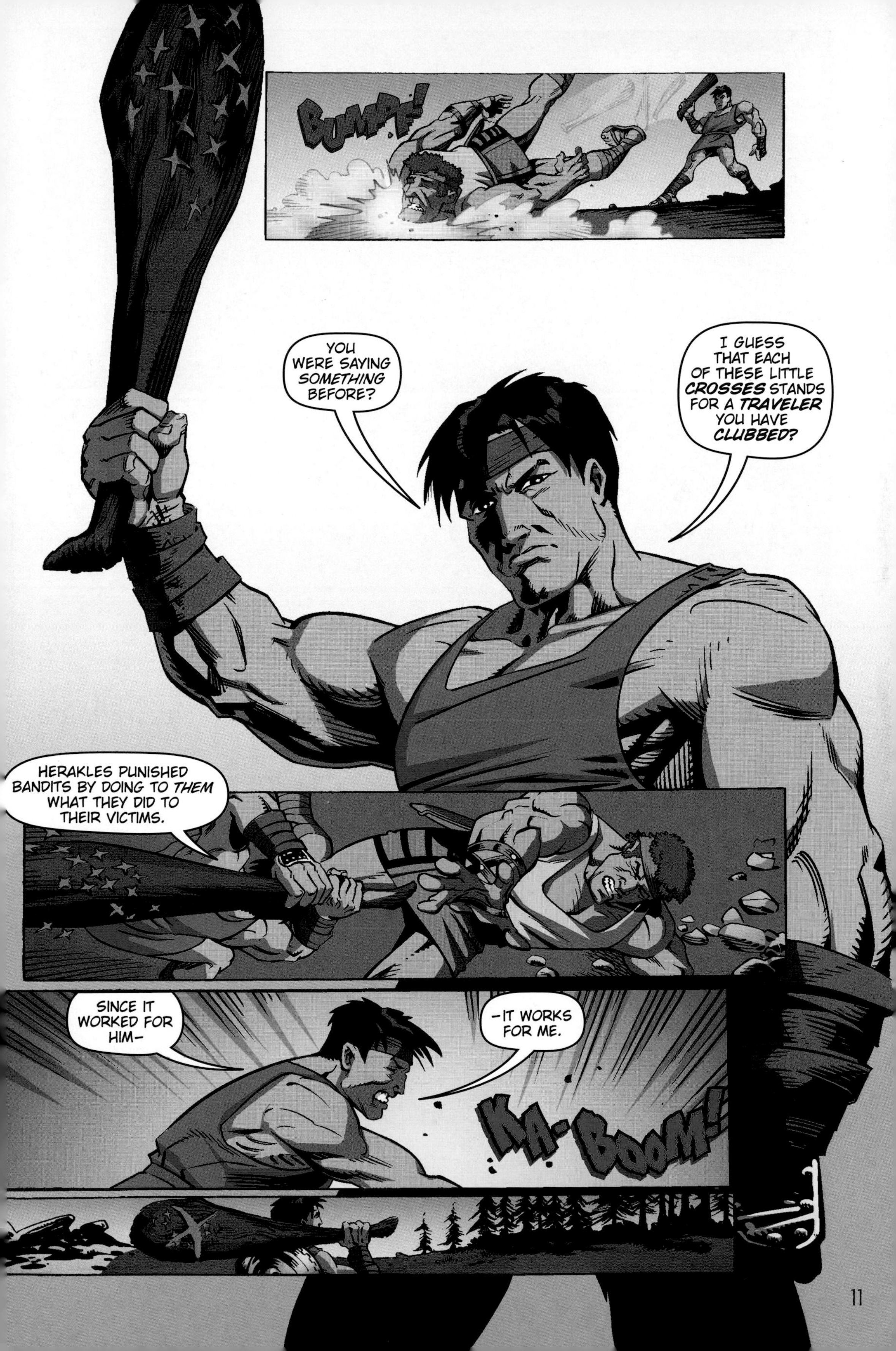
BUMPF!
YOU WERE SAYING SOMETHING BEFORE?
I GUESS THAT EACH OF THESE LITTLE CROSSES STANDS FOR A TRAVELER YOU HAVE CLUBBED?
HERAKLES PUNISHED BANDITS BY DOING TO THEM WHAT THEY DID TO THEIR VICTIMS.
SINCE IT WORKED FOR HIM-
-IT WORKS FOR ME.
KA-BOOM!

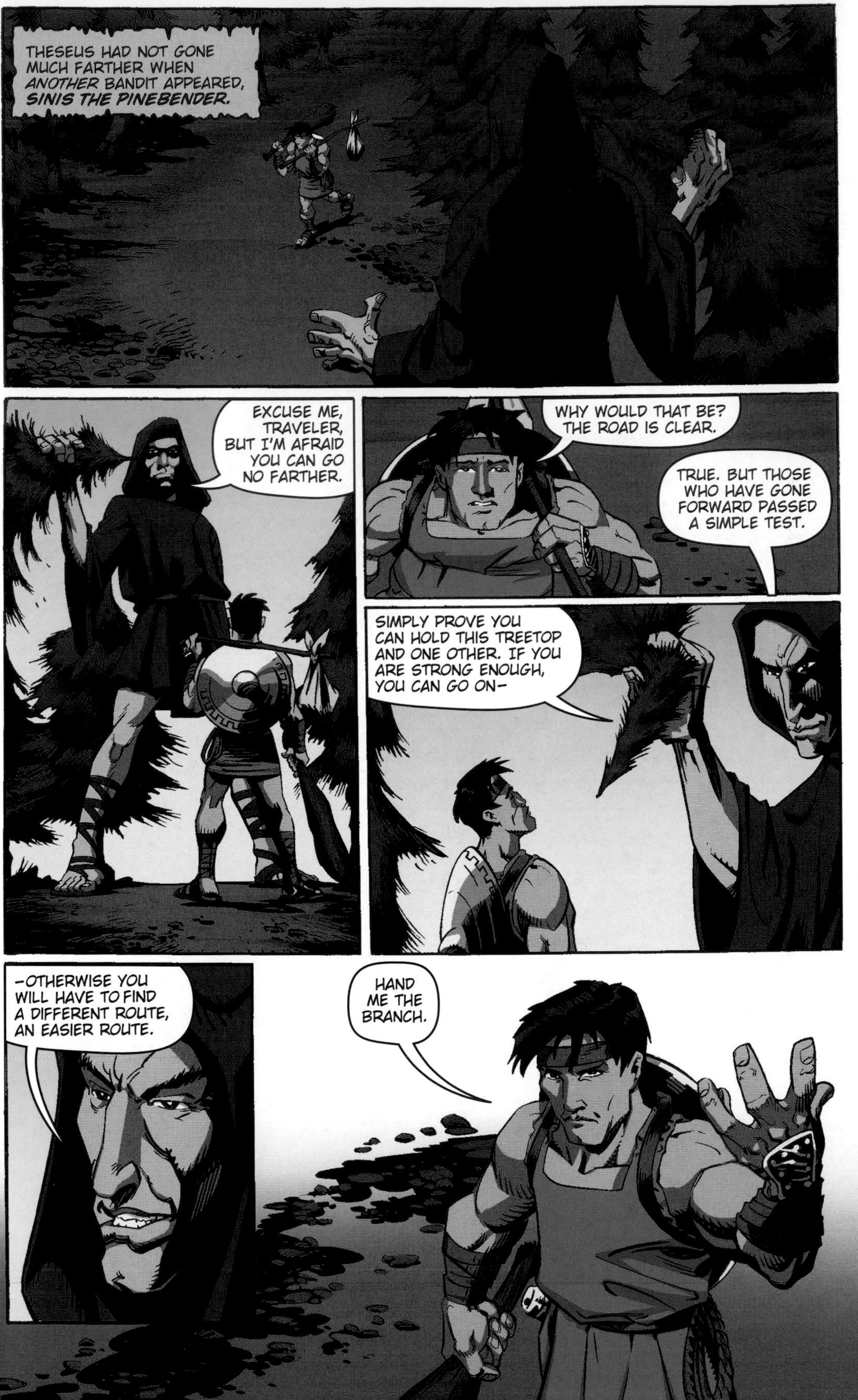
THESEUS HAD NOT GONE MUCH FARTHER WHEN *ANOTHER* BANDIT APPEARED, ***SINIS THE PINEBENDER.***
EXCUSE ME, TRAVELER, BUT I'M AFRAID YOU CAN GO NO FARTHER.
WHY WOULD THAT BE? THE ROAD IS CLEAR.
TRUE. BUT THOSE WHO HAVE GONE FORWARD PASSED A SIMPLE TEST.
SIMPLY PROVE YOU CAN HOLD THIS TREETOP AND ONE OTHER. IF YOU ARE STRONG ENOUGH, YOU CAN GO ON—
—OTHERWISE YOU WILL HAVE TO FIND A DIFFERENT ROUTE, AN EASIER ROUTE.
HAND ME THE BRANCH.

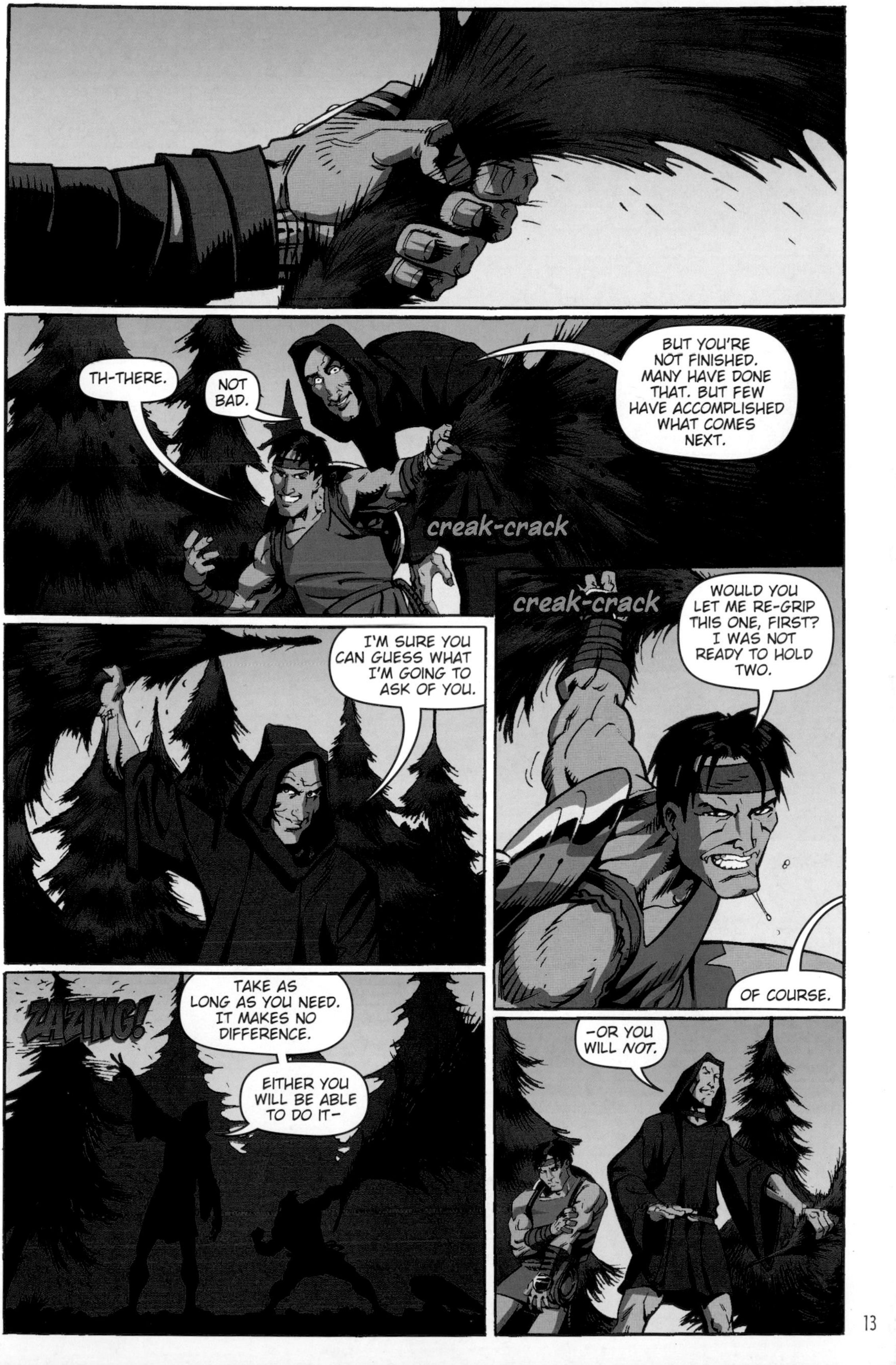

TH-THERE.
NOT BAD.
BUT YOU'RE NOT FINISHED. MANY HAVE DONE THAT. BUT FEW HAVE ACCOMPLISHED WHAT COMES NEXT.
creak-crack
creak-crack
I'M SURE YOU CAN GUESS WHAT I'M GOING TO ASK OF YOU.
WOULD YOU LET ME RE-GRIP THIS ONE, FIRST? I WAS NOT READY TO HOLD TWO.
OF COURSE.
ZAZING!
TAKE AS LONG AS YOU NEED. IT MAKES NO DIFFERENCE.
EITHER YOU WILL BE ABLE TO DO IT-
-OR YOU WILL *NOT*.

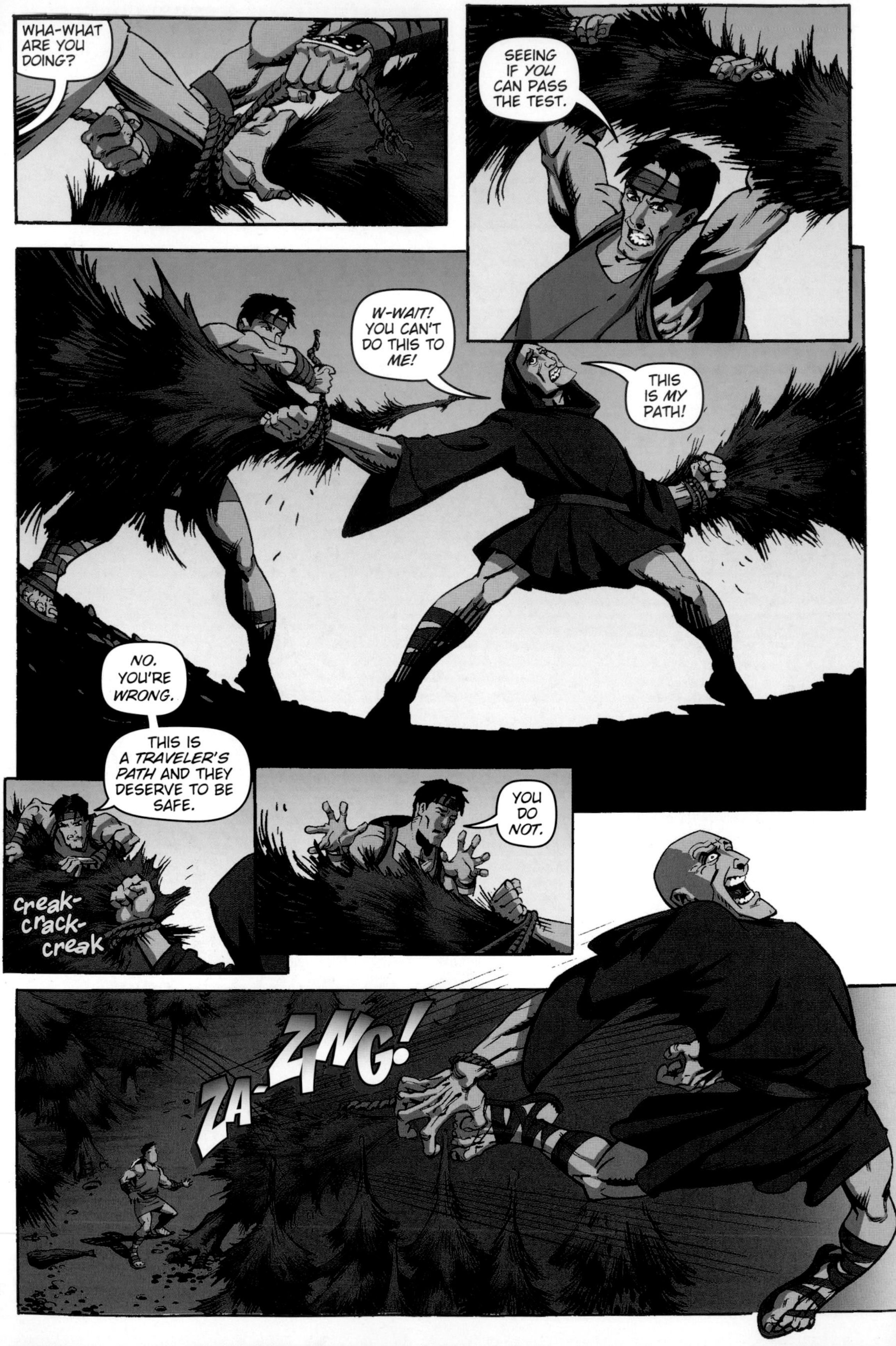
WHA-WHAT ARE YOU DOING?
SEEING IF YOU CAN PASS THE TEST.
W-WAIT! YOU CAN'T DO THIS TO ME!
THIS IS MY PATH!
NO. YOU'RE WRONG.
THIS IS A TRAVELER'S PATH AND THEY DESERVE TO BE SAFE.
YOU DO NOT.
creak-crack-creak
ZA-ZING!

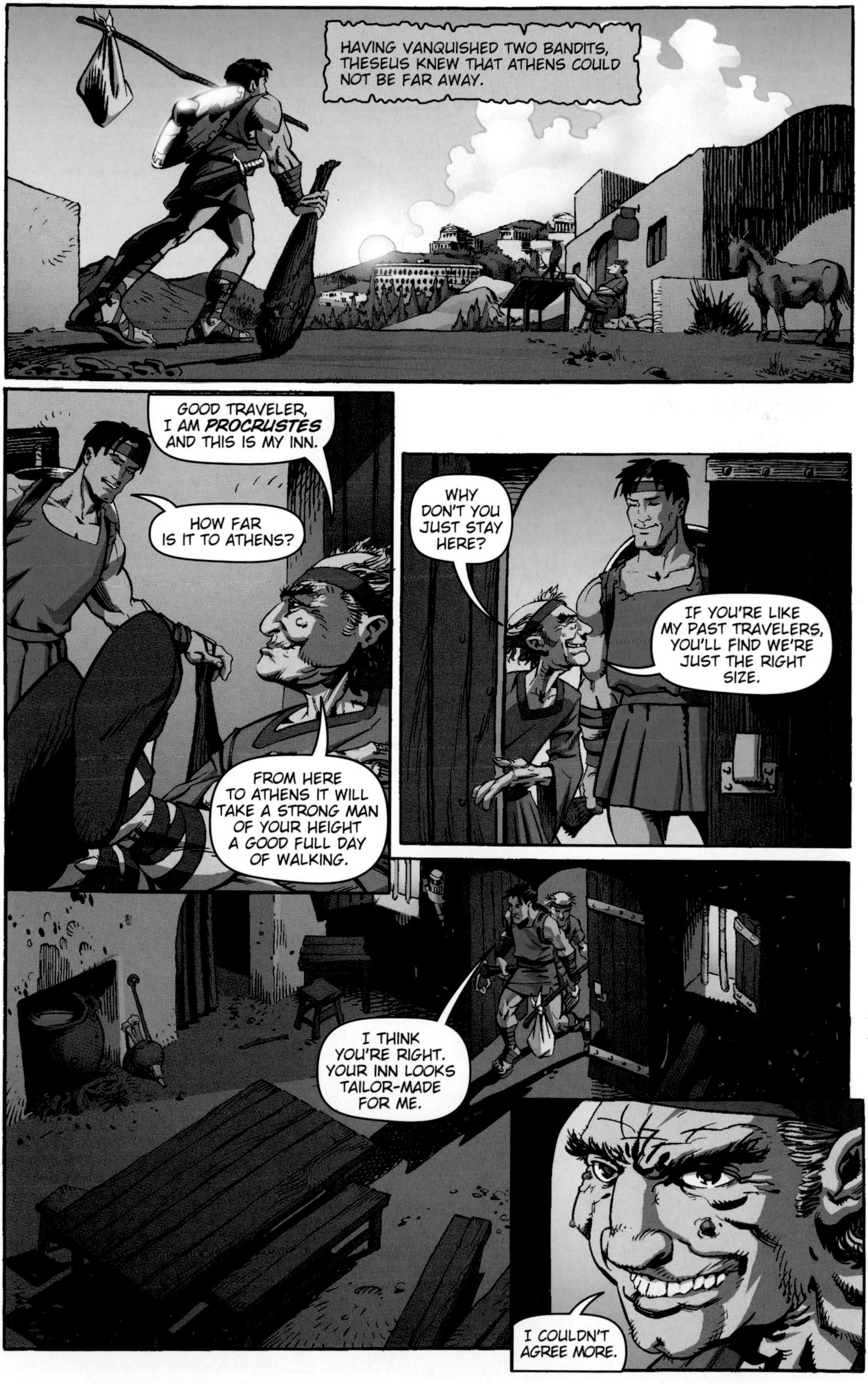
HAVING VANQUISHED TWO BANDITS, THESEUS KNEW THAT ATHENS COULD NOT BE FAR AWAY.
GOOD TRAVELER, I AM PROCRUSTES AND THIS IS MY INN.
HOW FAR IS IT TO ATHENS?
FROM HERE TO ATHENS IT WILL TAKE A STRONG MAN OF YOUR HEIGHT A GOOD FULL DAY OF WALKING.
WHY DON'T YOU JUST STAY HERE?
IF YOU'RE LIKE MY PAST TRAVELERS, YOU'LL FIND WE'RE JUST THE RIGHT SIZE.
I THINK YOU'RE RIGHT. YOUR INN LOOKS TAILOR-MADE FOR ME.
I COULDN'T AGREE MORE.

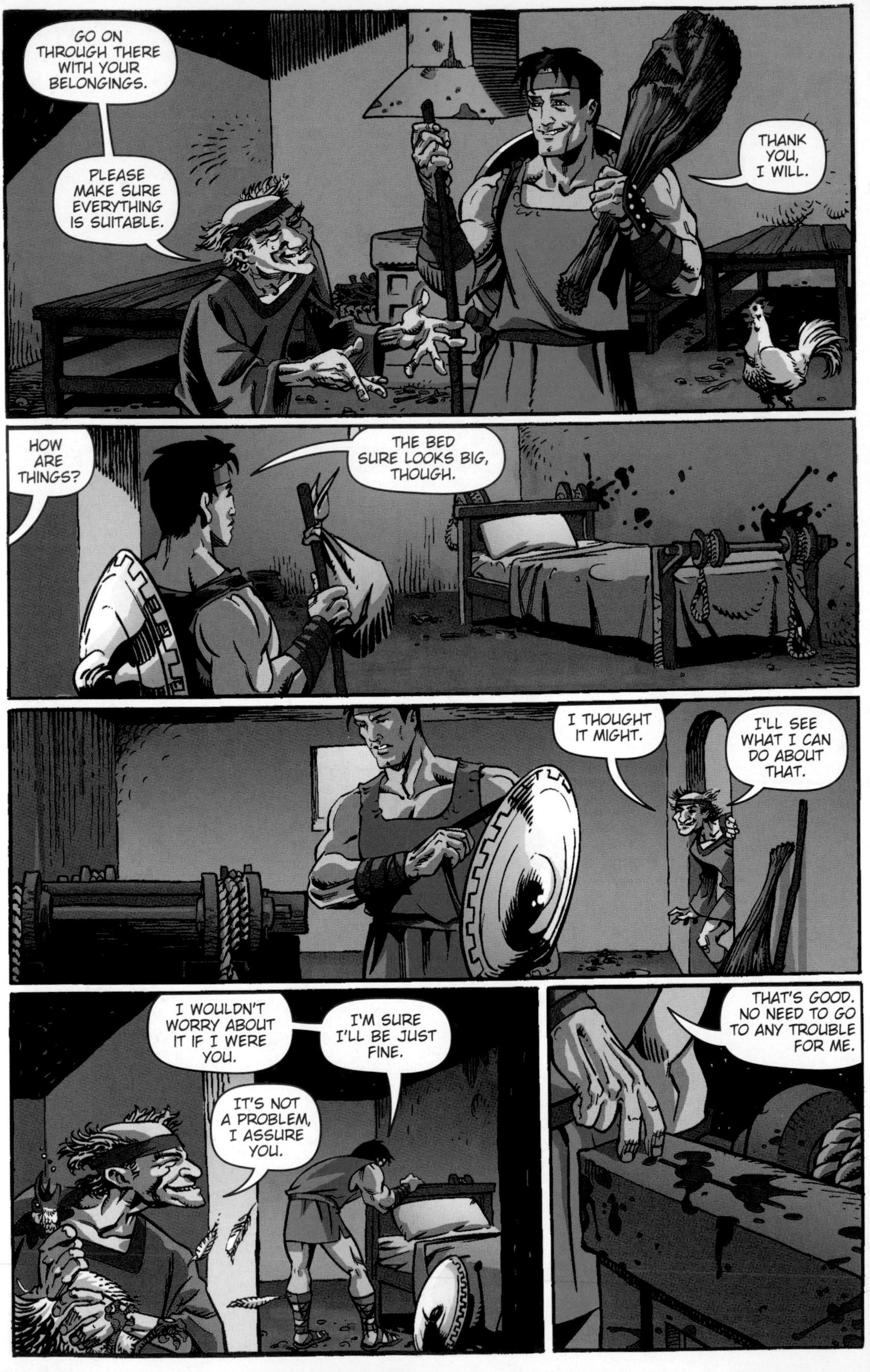
GO ON THROUGH THERE WITH YOUR BELONGINGS.
PLEASE MAKE SURE EVERYTHING IS SUITABLE.
THANK YOU, I WILL.
HOW ARE THINGS?
THE BED SURE LOOKS BIG, THOUGH.
I THOUGHT IT MIGHT.
I'LL SEE WHAT I CAN DO ABOUT THAT.
I WOULDN'T WORRY ABOUT IT IF I WERE YOU.
I'M SURE I'LL BE JUST FINE.
IT'S NOT A PROBLEM, I ASSURE YOU.
THAT'S GOOD. NO NEED TO GO TO ANY TROUBLE FOR ME.

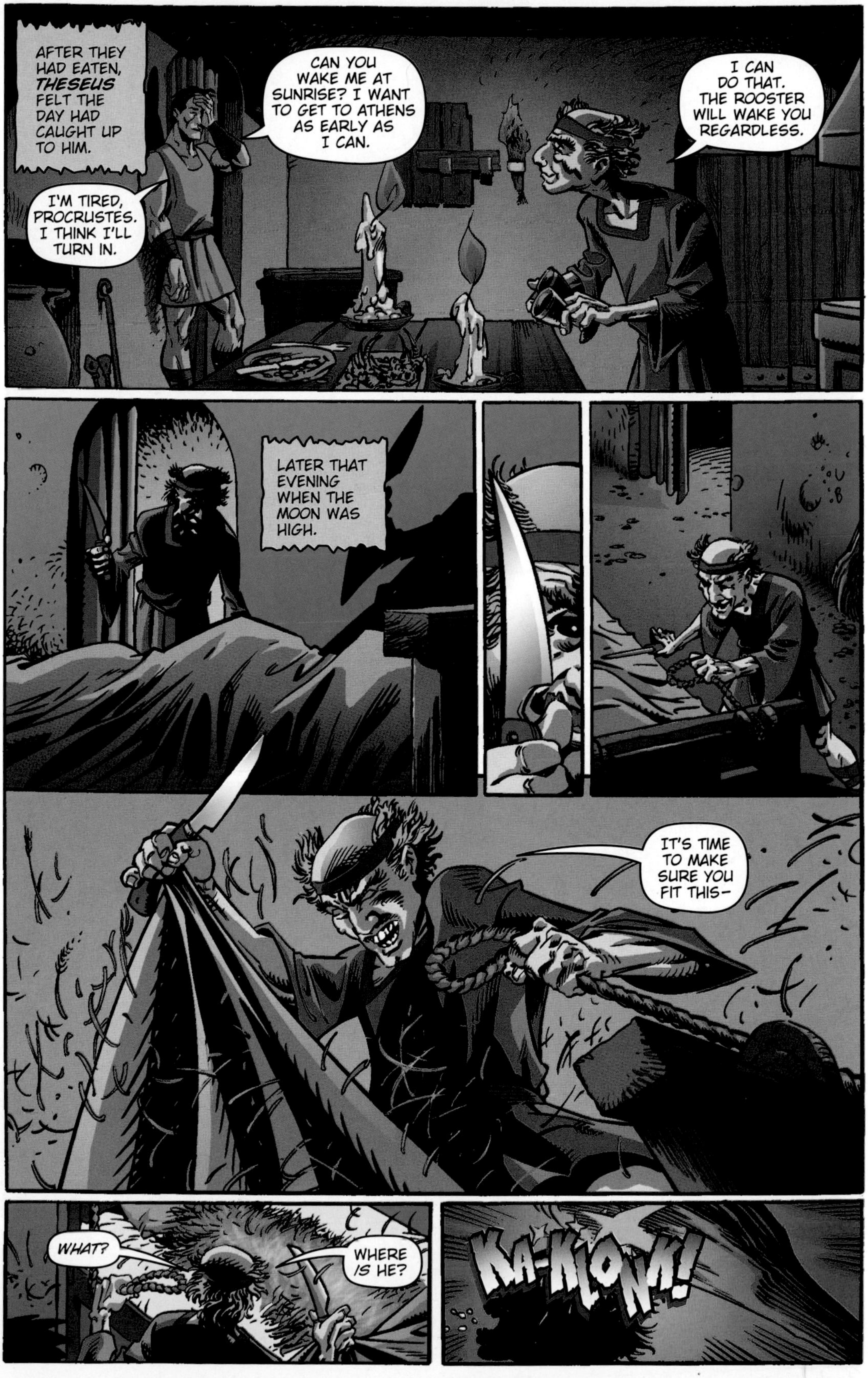
AFTER THEY HAD EATEN, THESEUS FELT THE DAY HAD CAUGHT UP TO HIM.
I'M TIRED, PROCRUSTES. I THINK I'LL TURN IN.
CAN YOU WAKE ME AT SUNRISE? I WANT TO GET TO ATHENS AS EARLY AS I CAN.
I CAN DO THAT. THE ROOSTER WILL WAKE YOU REGARDLESS.
LATER THAT EVENING WHEN THE MOON WAS HIGH.
IT'S TIME TO MAKE SURE YOU FIT THIS—
WHAT?
WHERE IS HE?
KA-KLONK!

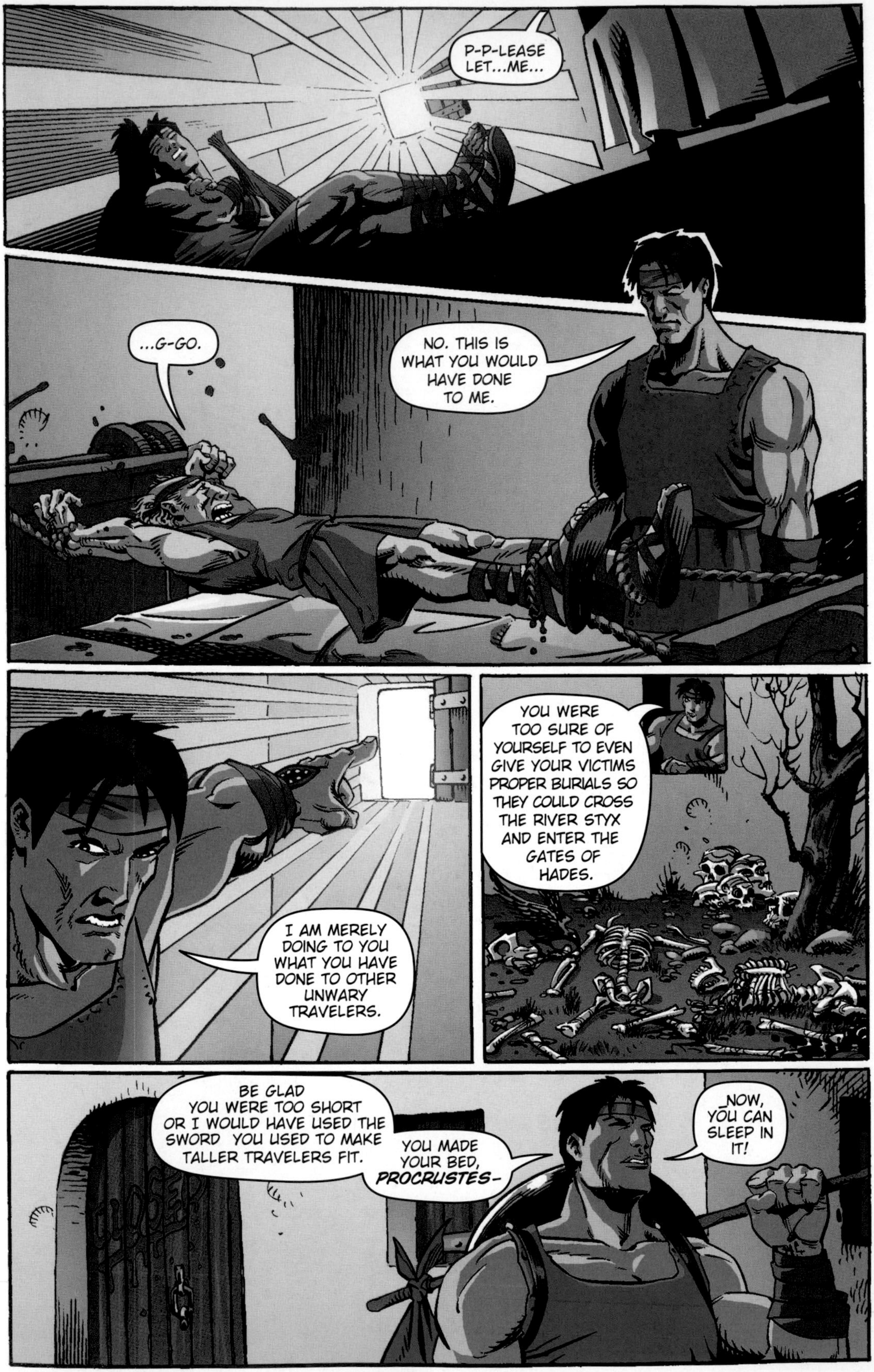
P-P-LEASE LET...ME...
...G-GO.
NO. THIS IS WHAT YOU WOULD HAVE DONE TO ME.
I AM MERELY DOING TO YOU WHAT YOU HAVE DONE TO OTHER UNWARY TRAVELERS.
YOU WERE TOO SURE OF YOURSELF TO EVEN GIVE YOUR VICTIMS PROPER BURIALS SO THEY COULD CROSS THE RIVER STYX AND ENTER THE GATES OF HADES.
BE GLAD YOU WERE TOO SHORT OR I WOULD HAVE USED THE SWORD YOU USED TO MAKE TALLER TRAVELERS FIT.
YOU MADE YOUR BED, *PROCRUSTES*-
_NOW, YOU CAN SLEEP IN IT!

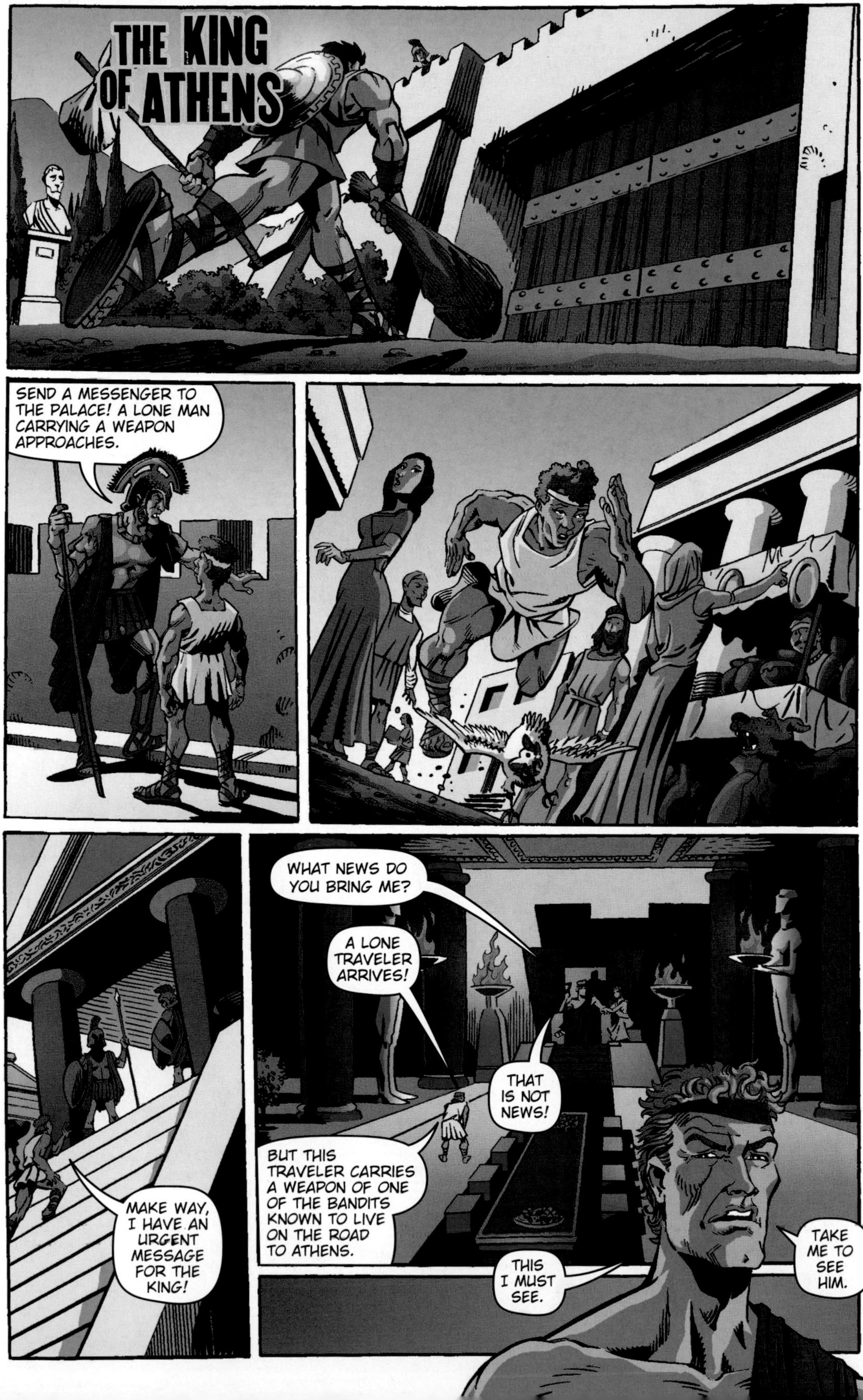
THE KING OF ATHENS
SEND A MESSENGER TO THE PALACE! A LONE MAN CARRYING A WEAPON APPROACHES.
MAKE WAY, I HAVE AN URGENT MESSAGE FOR THE KING!
WHAT NEWS DO YOU BRING ME?
A LONE TRAVELER ARRIVES!
THAT IS NOT NEWS!
BUT THIS TRAVELER CARRIES A WEAPON OF ONE OF THE BANDITS KNOWN TO LIVE ON THE ROAD TO ATHENS.
THIS I MUST SEE.
TAKE ME TO SEE HIM.

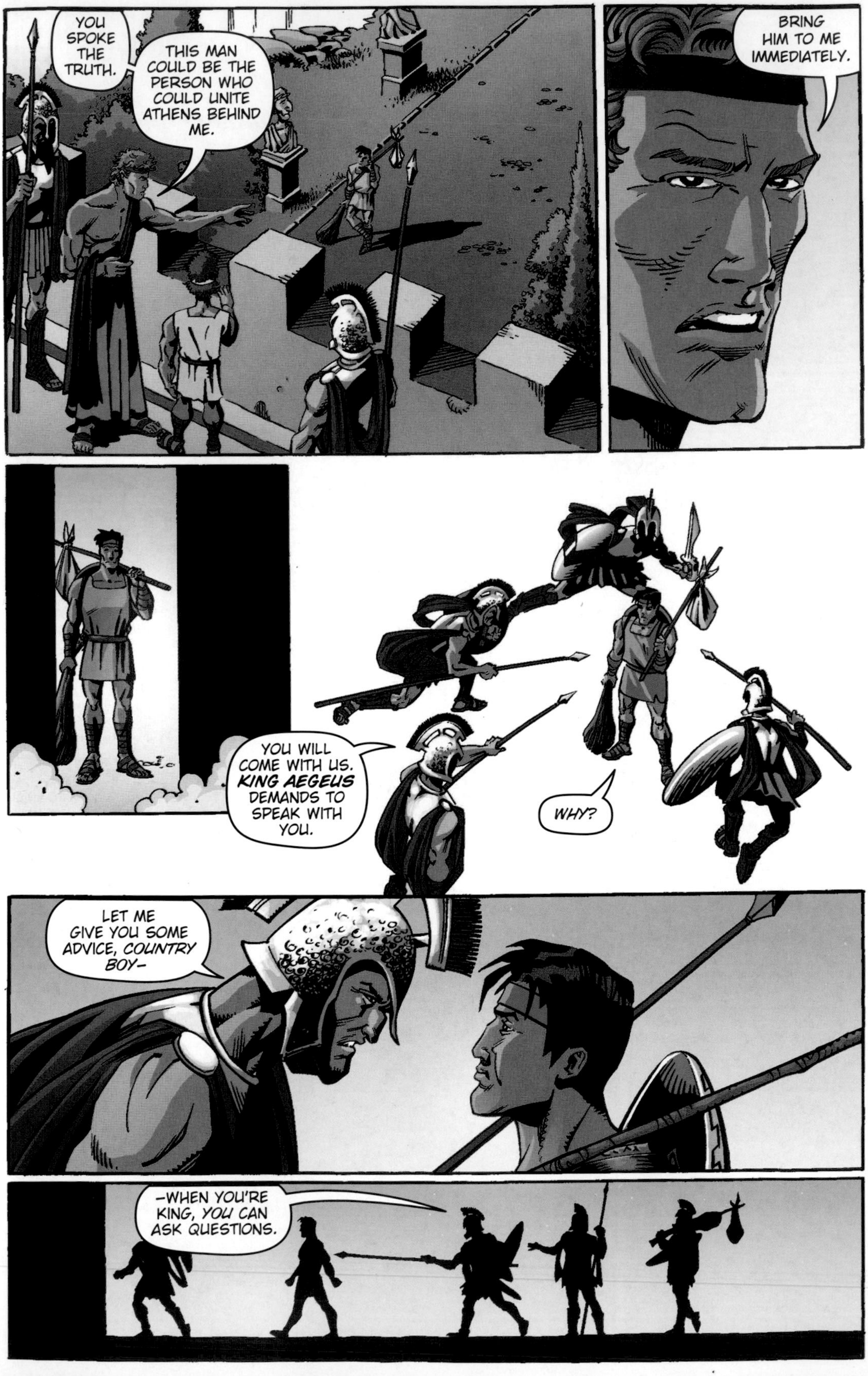

YOU SPOKE THE TRUTH.
THIS MAN COULD BE THE PERSON WHO COULD UNITE ATHENS BEHIND ME.
BRING HIM TO ME IMMEDIATELY.
YOU WILL COME WITH US. KING AEGEUS DEMANDS TO SPEAK WITH YOU.
WHY?
LET ME GIVE YOU SOME ADVICE, COUNTRY BOY-
-WHEN YOU'RE KING, YOU CAN ASK QUESTIONS.

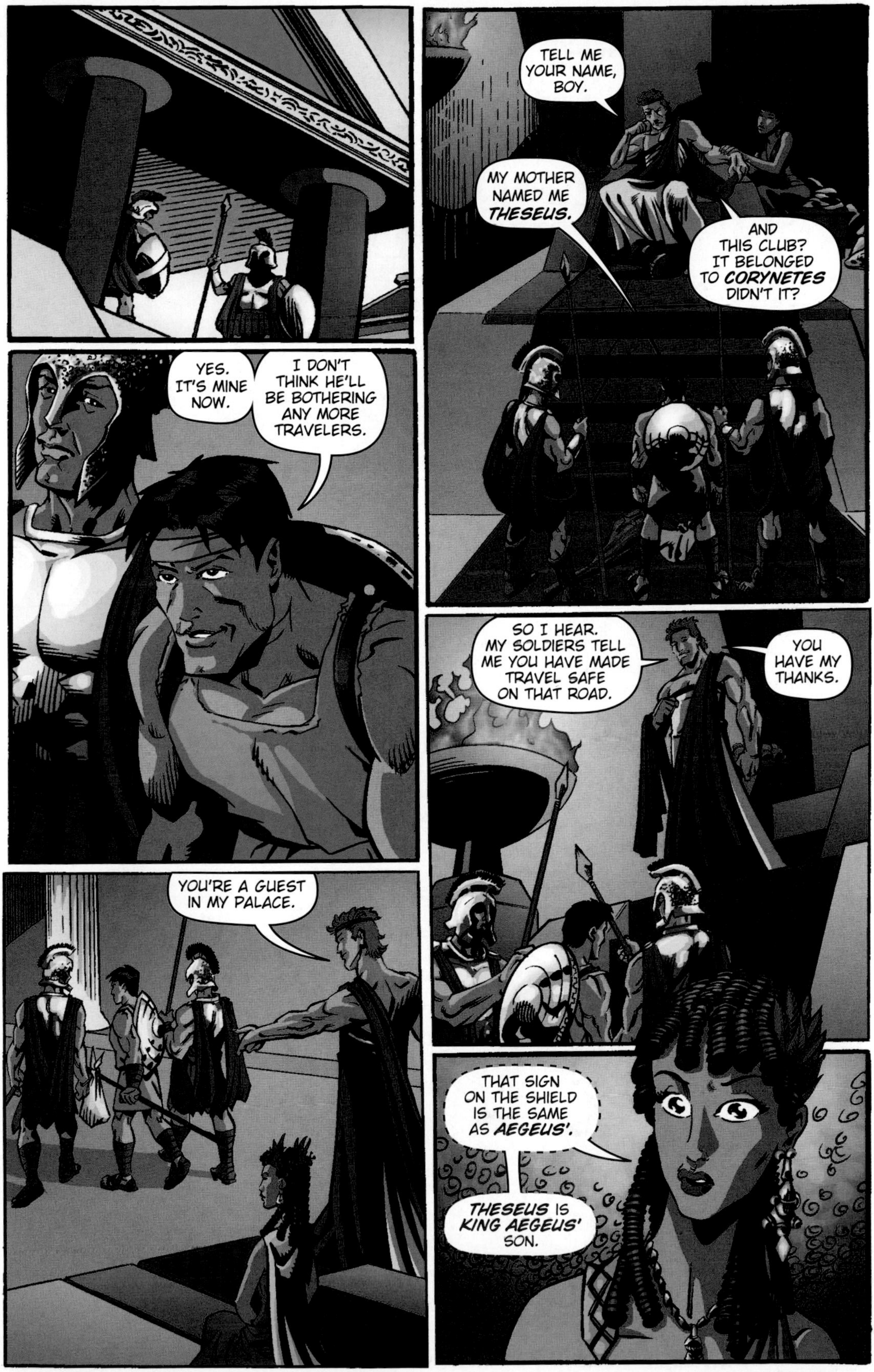

TELL ME YOUR NAME, BOY.
MY MOTHER NAMED ME THESEUS.
AND THIS CLUB? IT BELONGED TO CORYNETES DIDN'T IT?
YES. IT'S MINE NOW.
I DON'T THINK HE'LL BE BOTHERING ANY MORE TRAVELERS.
SO I HEAR. MY SOLDIERS TELL ME YOU HAVE MADE TRAVEL SAFE ON THAT ROAD.
YOU HAVE MY THANKS.
YOU'RE A GUEST IN MY PALACE.
THAT SIGN ON THE SHIELD IS THE SAME AS AEGEUS'.
THESEUS IS KING AEGEUS' SON.

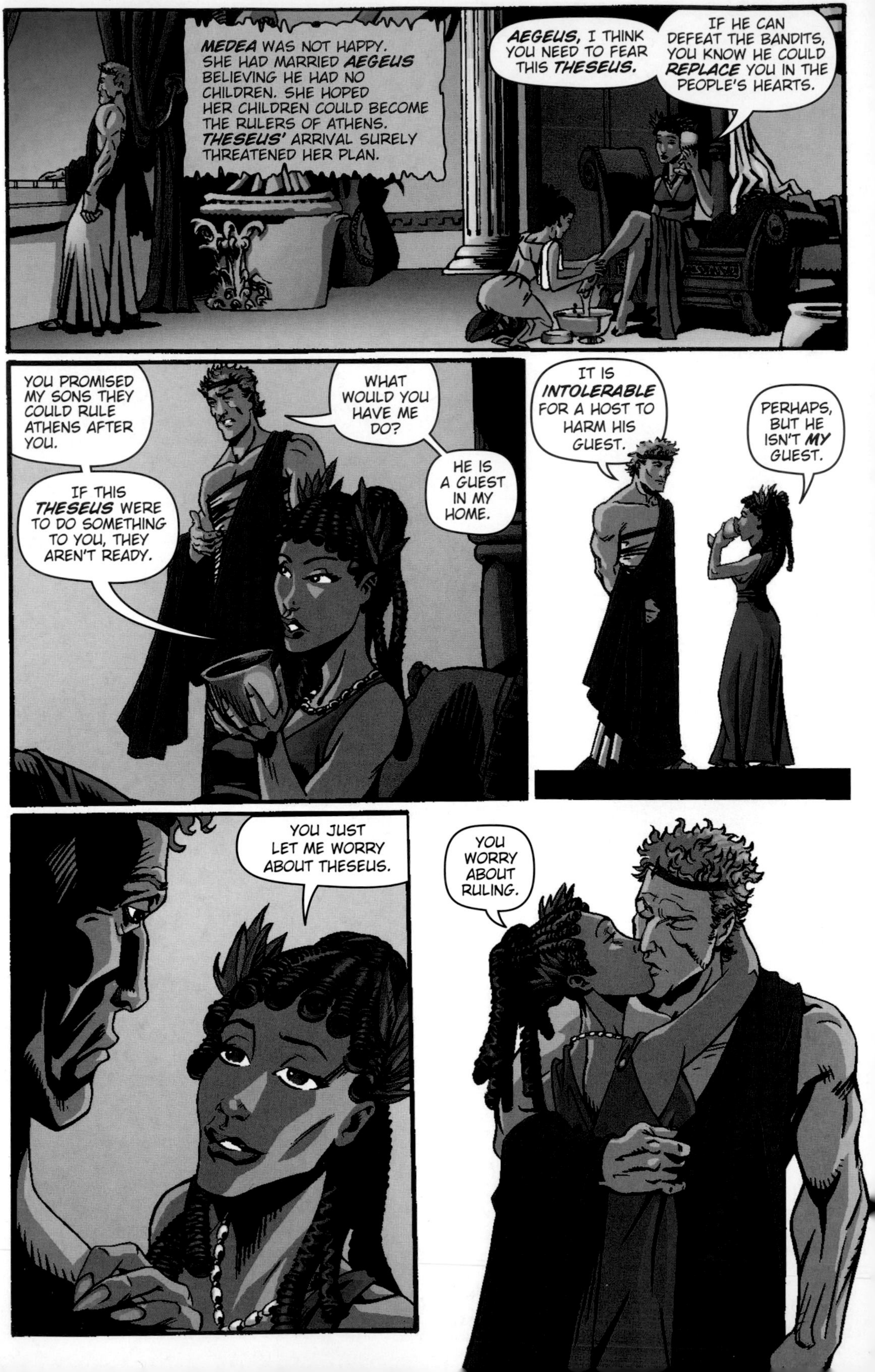
MEDEA WAS NOT HAPPY. SHE HAD MARRIED AEGEUS BELIEVING HE HAD NO CHILDREN. SHE HOPED HER CHILDREN COULD BECOME THE RULERS OF ATHENS. THESEUS' ARRIVAL SURELY THREATENED HER PLAN.
AEGEUS, I THINK YOU NEED TO FEAR THIS THESEUS.
IF HE CAN DEFEAT THE BANDITS, YOU KNOW HE COULD REPLACE YOU IN THE PEOPLE'S HEARTS.
YOU PROMISED MY SONS THEY COULD RULE ATHENS AFTER YOU.
WHAT WOULD YOU HAVE ME DO?
HE IS A GUEST IN MY HOME.
IF THIS THESEUS WERE TO DO SOMETHING TO YOU, THEY AREN'T READY.
IT IS INTOLERABLE FOR A HOST TO HARM HIS GUEST.
PERHAPS, BUT HE ISN'T MY GUEST.
YOU JUST LET ME WORRY ABOUT THESEUS.
YOU WORRY ABOUT RULING.

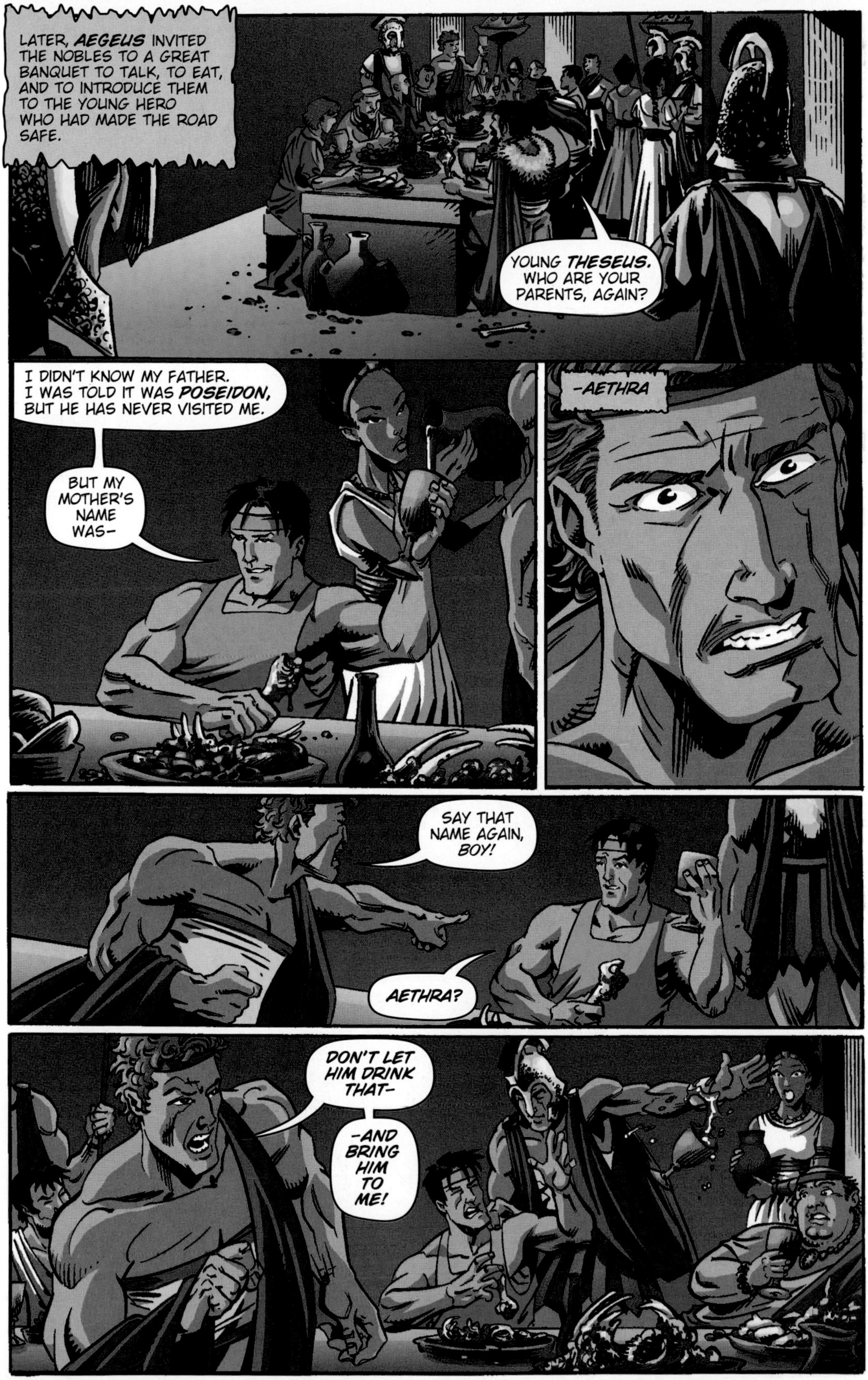
LATER, AEGEUS INVITED THE NOBLES TO A GREAT BANQUET TO TALK, TO EAT, AND TO INTRODUCE THEM TO THE YOUNG HERO WHO HAD MADE THE ROAD SAFE.
YOUNG THESEUS. WHO ARE YOUR PARENTS, AGAIN?
I DIDN'T KNOW MY FATHER. I WAS TOLD IT WAS POSEIDON, BUT HE HAS NEVER VISITED ME.
BUT MY MOTHER'S NAME WAS-
-AETHRA
SAY THAT NAME AGAIN, BOY!
AETHRA?
DON'T LET HIM DRINK THAT-
-AND BRING HIM TO ME!

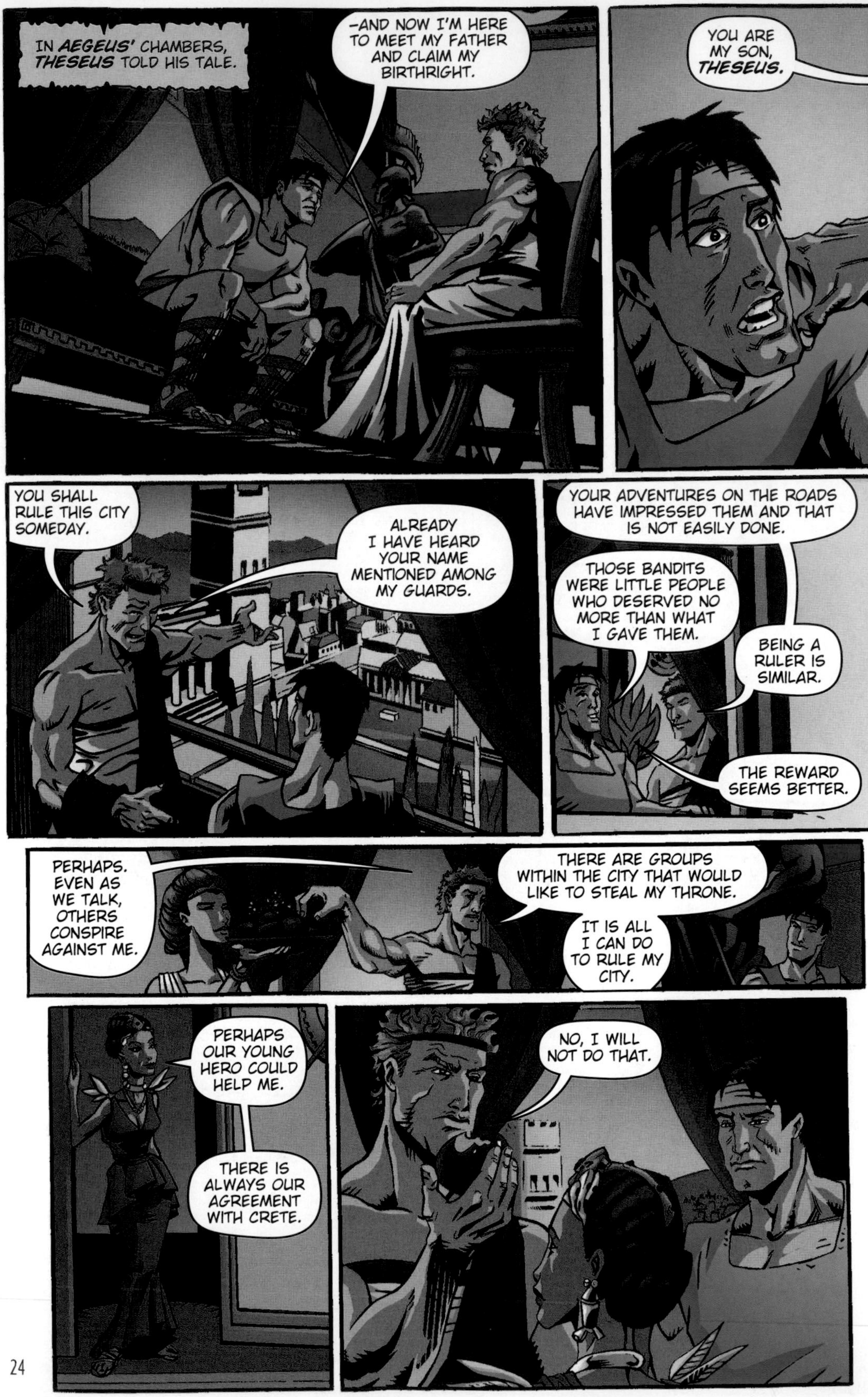
IN AEGEUS' CHAMBERS, THESEUS TOLD HIS TALE.
—AND NOW I'M HERE TO MEET MY FATHER AND CLAIM MY BIRTHRIGHT.
YOU ARE MY SON, THESEUS.
YOU SHALL RULE THIS CITY SOMEDAY.
ALREADY I HAVE HEARD YOUR NAME MENTIONED AMONG MY GUARDS.
YOUR ADVENTURES ON THE ROADS HAVE IMPRESSED THEM AND THAT IS NOT EASILY DONE.
THOSE BANDITS WERE LITTLE PEOPLE WHO DESERVED NO MORE THAN WHAT I GAVE THEM.
BEING A RULER IS SIMILAR.
THE REWARD SEEMS BETTER.
PERHAPS. EVEN AS WE TALK, OTHERS CONSPIRE AGAINST ME.
THERE ARE GROUPS WITHIN THE CITY THAT WOULD LIKE TO STEAL MY THRONE.
IT IS ALL I CAN DO TO RULE MY CITY.
PERHAPS OUR YOUNG HERO COULD HELP ME.
THERE IS ALWAYS OUR AGREEMENT WITH CRETE.
NO, I WILL NOT DO THAT.

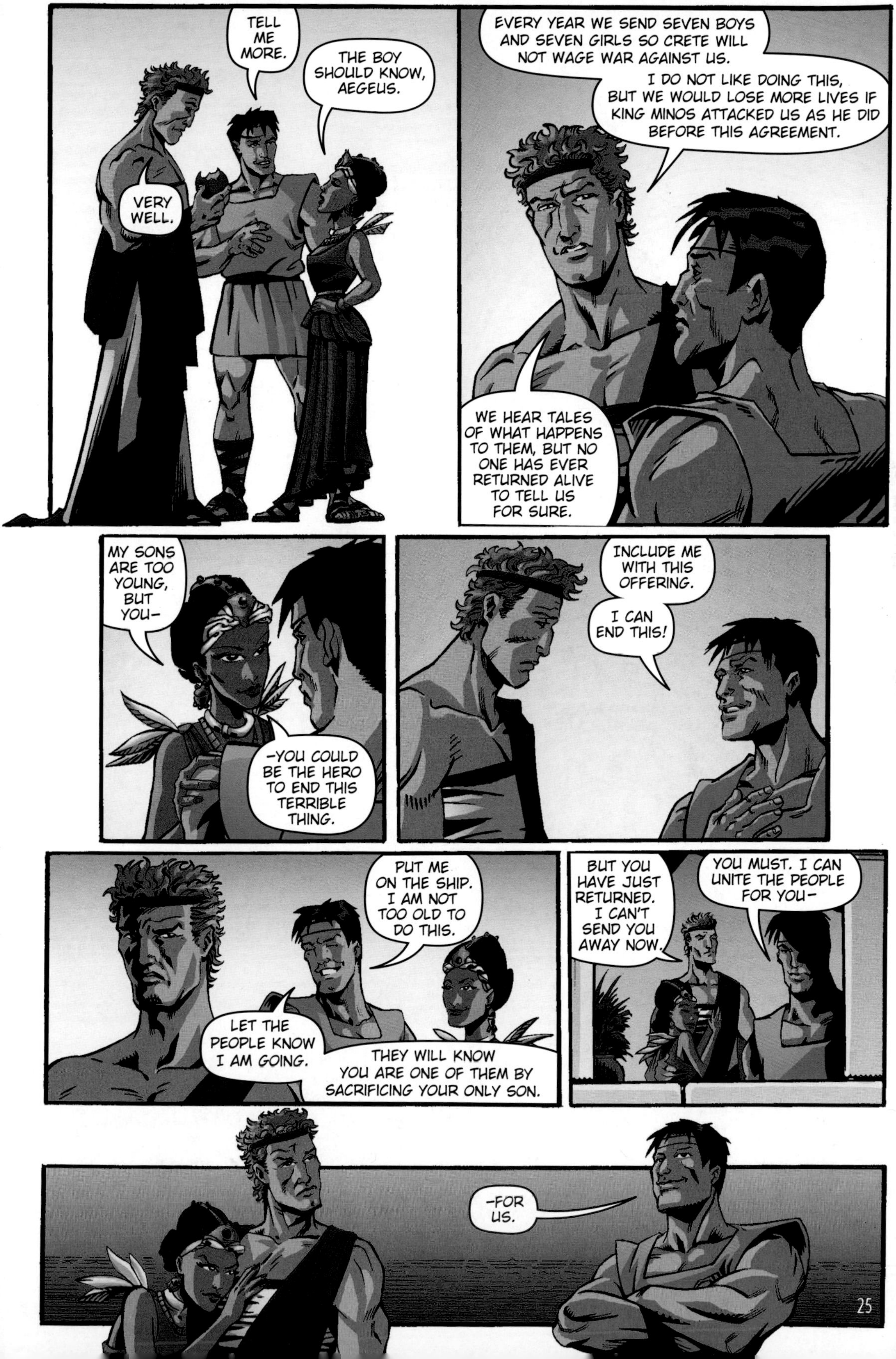
TELL ME MORE.
THE BOY SHOULD KNOW, AEGEUS.
VERY WELL.
EVERY YEAR WE SEND SEVEN BOYS AND SEVEN GIRLS SO CRETE WILL NOT WAGE WAR AGAINST US.
I DO NOT LIKE DOING THIS, BUT WE WOULD LOSE MORE LIVES IF KING MINOS ATTACKED US AS HE DID BEFORE THIS AGREEMENT.
WE HEAR TALES OF WHAT HAPPENS TO THEM, BUT NO ONE HAS EVER RETURNED ALIVE TO TELL US FOR SURE.
MY SONS ARE TOO YOUNG, BUT YOU–
–YOU COULD BE THE HERO TO END THIS TERRIBLE THING.
INCLUDE ME WITH THIS OFFERING.
I CAN END THIS!
PUT ME ON THE SHIP. I AM NOT TOO OLD TO DO THIS.
LET THE PEOPLE KNOW I AM GOING.
THEY WILL KNOW YOU ARE ONE OF THEM BY SACRIFICING YOUR ONLY SON.
BUT YOU HAVE JUST RETURNED. I CAN'T SEND YOU AWAY NOW.
YOU MUST. I CAN UNITE THE PEOPLE FOR YOU–
–FOR US.

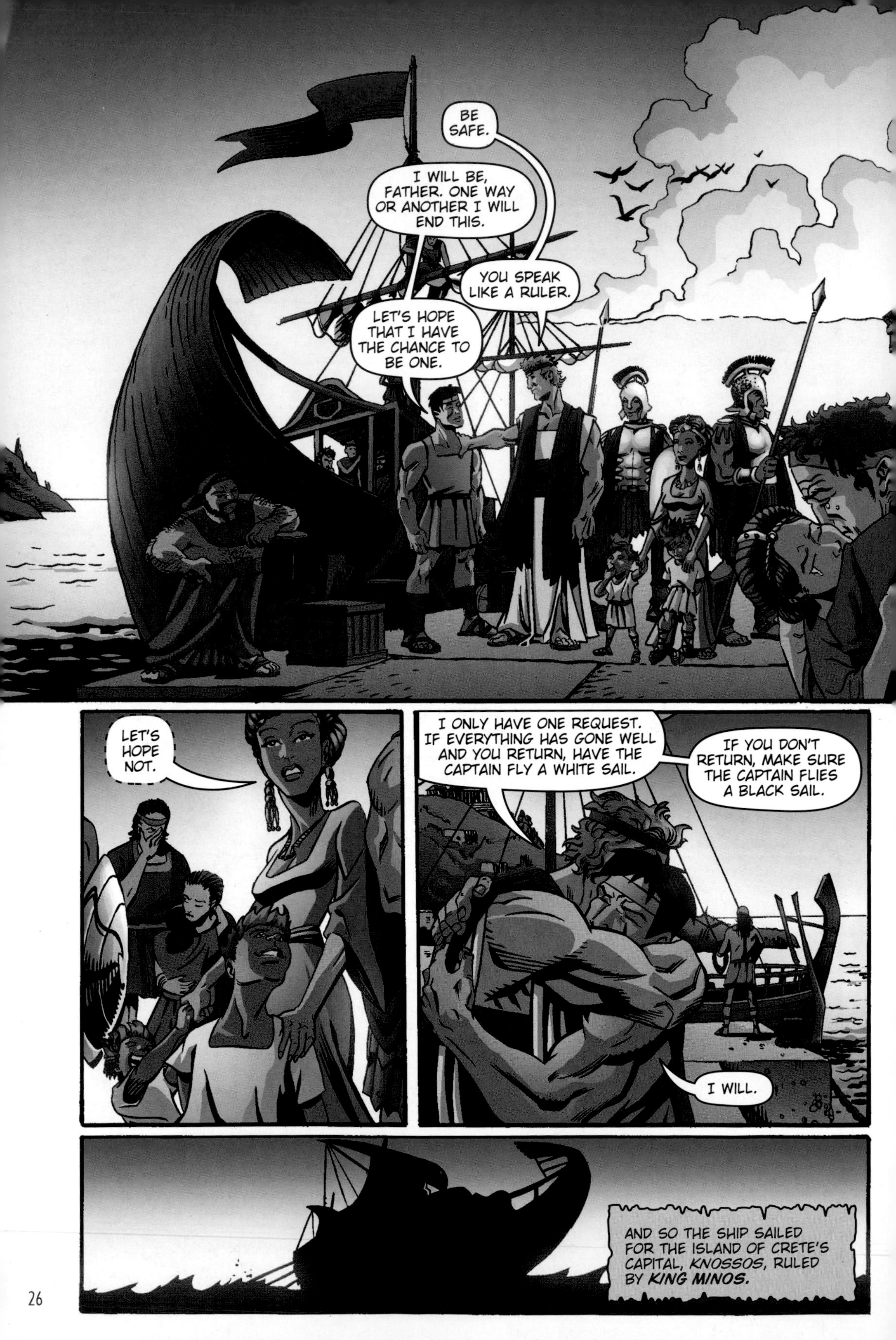
BE SAFE.
I WILL BE, FATHER. ONE WAY OR ANOTHER I WILL END THIS.
YOU SPEAK LIKE A RULER.
LET'S HOPE THAT I HAVE THE CHANCE TO BE ONE.
LET'S HOPE NOT.
I ONLY HAVE ONE REQUEST. IF EVERYTHING HAS GONE WELL AND YOU RETURN, HAVE THE CAPTAIN FLY A WHITE SAIL.
IF YOU DON'T RETURN, MAKE SURE THE CAPTAIN FLIES A BLACK SAIL.
I WILL.
AND SO THE SHIP SAILED FOR THE ISLAND OF CRETE'S CAPITAL, KNOSSOS, RULED BY KING MINOS.

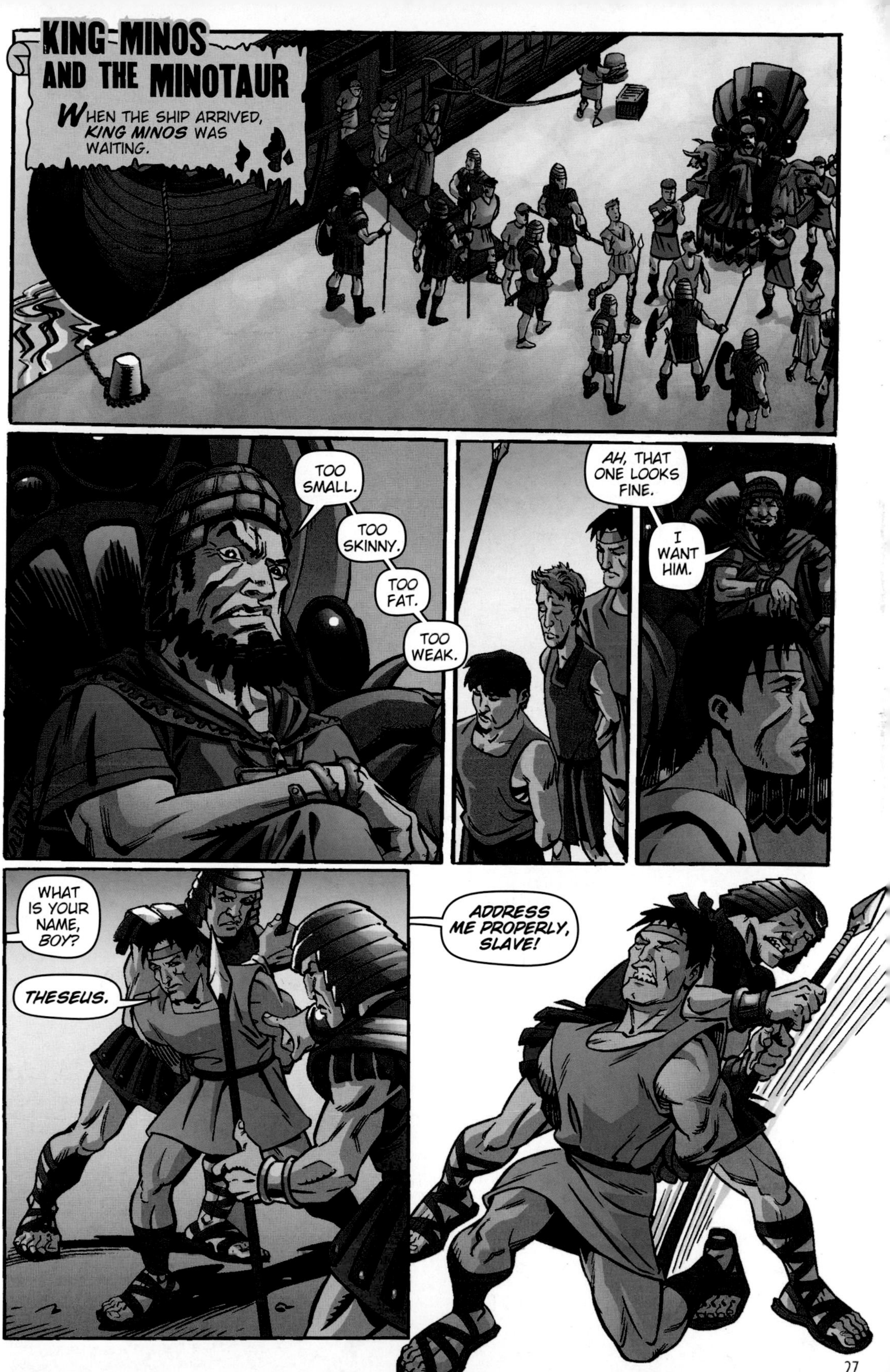
KING MINOS AND THE MINOTAUR
WHEN THE SHIP ARRIVED, KING MINOS WAS WAITING.
TOO SMALL.
TOO SKINNY.
TOO FAT.
TOO WEAK.
AH, THAT ONE LOOKS FINE.
I WANT HIM.
WHAT IS YOUR NAME, BOY?
THESEUS.
ADDRESS ME PROPERLY, SLAVE!

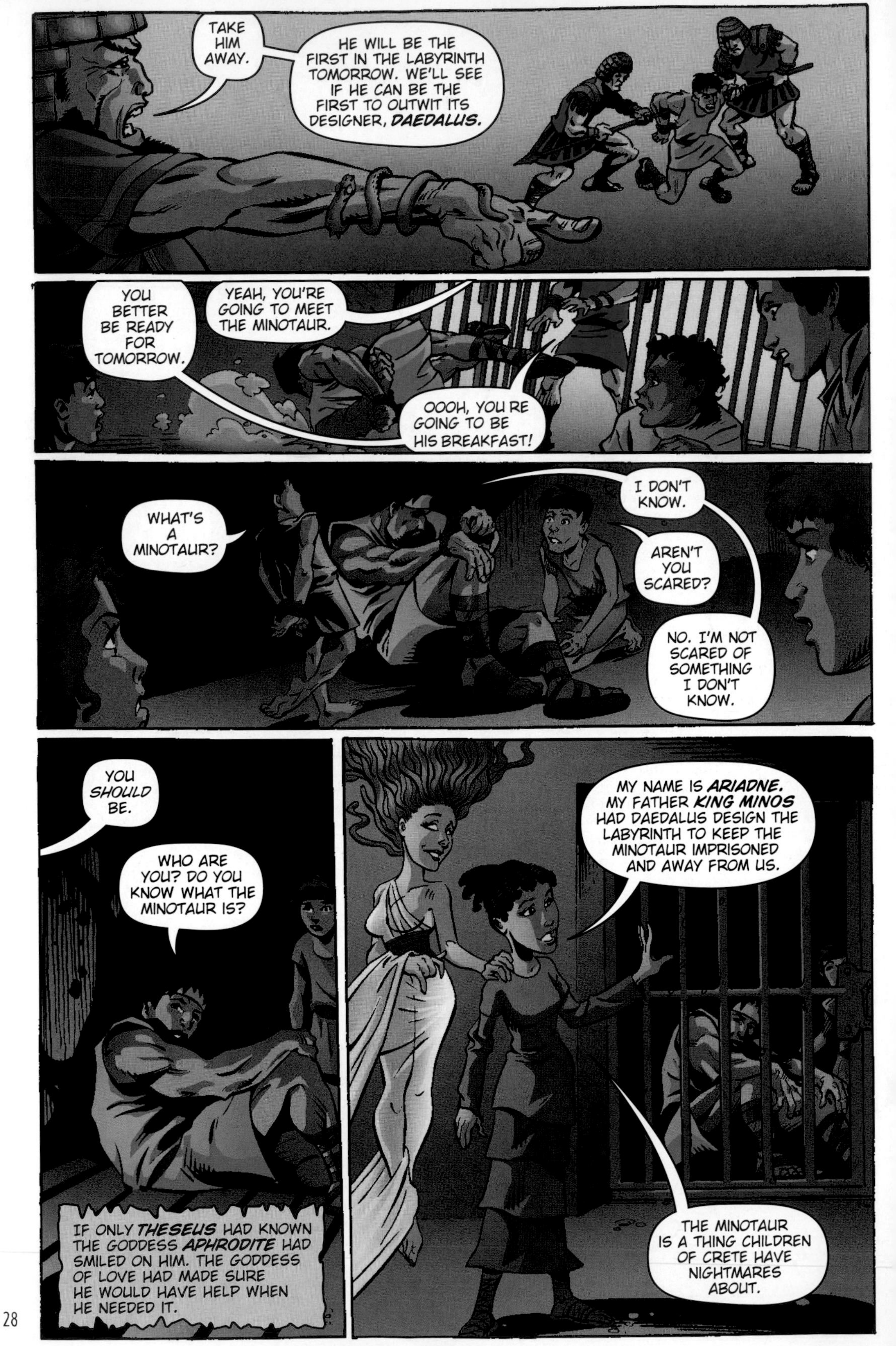
TAKE HIM AWAY.
HE WILL BE THE FIRST IN THE LABYRINTH TOMORROW. WE'LL SEE IF HE CAN BE THE FIRST TO OUTWIT ITS DESIGNER, DAEDALUS.
YOU BETTER BE READY FOR TOMORROW.
YEAH, YOU'RE GOING TO MEET THE MINOTAUR.
OOOH, YOU RE GOING TO BE HIS BREAKFAST!
WHAT'S A MINOTAUR?
I DON'T KNOW.
AREN'T YOU SCARED?
NO. I'M NOT SCARED OF SOMETHING I DON'T KNOW.
YOU SHOULD BE.
WHO ARE YOU? DO YOU KNOW WHAT THE MINOTAUR IS?
IF ONLY THESEUS HAD KNOWN THE GODDESS APHRODITE HAD SMILED ON HIM. THE GODDESS OF LOVE HAD MADE SURE HE WOULD HAVE HELP WHEN HE NEEDED IT.
MY NAME IS ARIADNE. MY FATHER KING MINOS HAD DAEDALUS DESIGN THE LABYRINTH TO KEEP THE MINOTAUR IMPRISONED AND AWAY FROM US.
THE MINOTAUR IS A THING CHILDREN OF CRETE HAVE NIGHTMARES ABOUT.

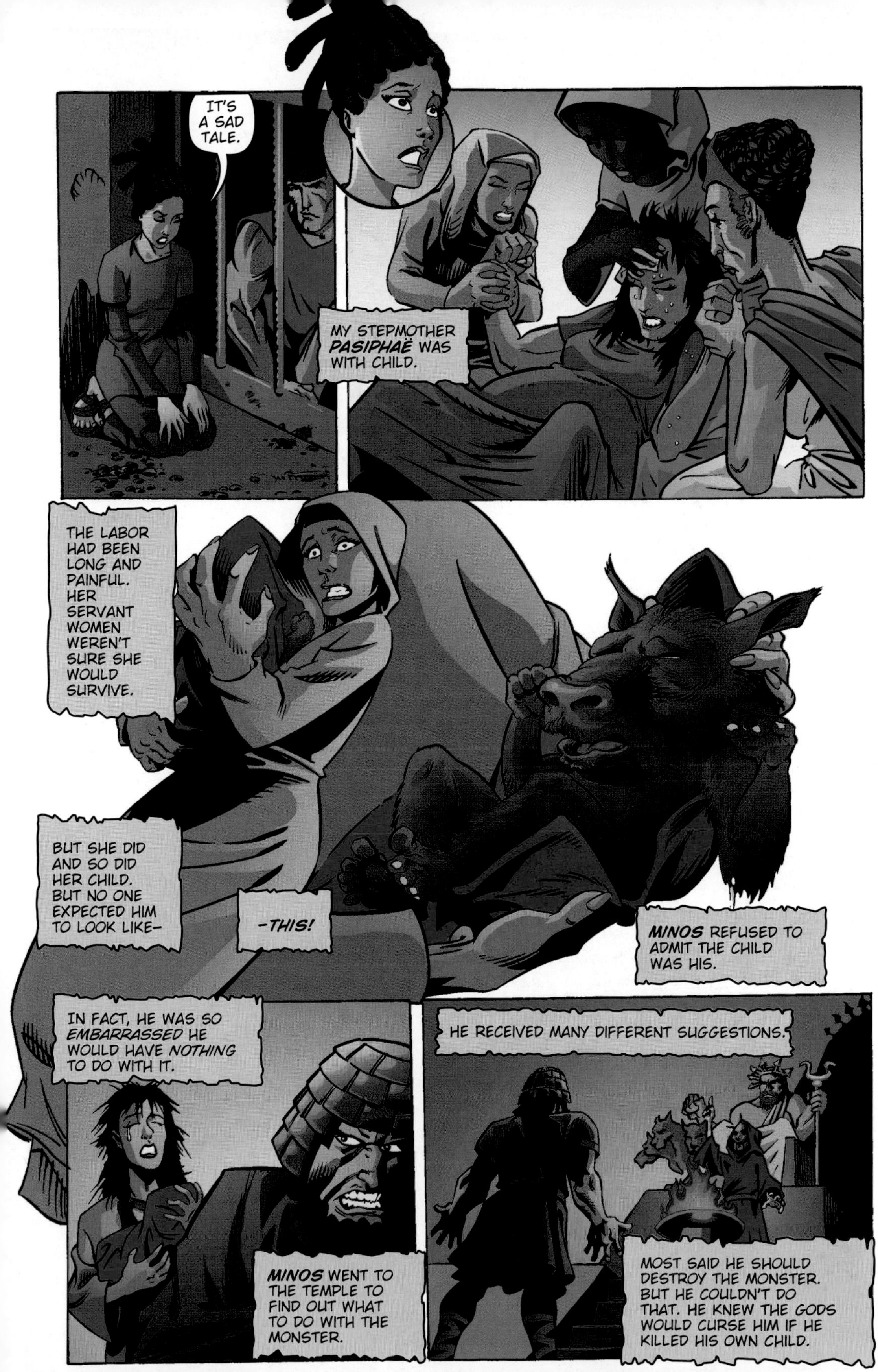
IT'S A SAD TALE.
MY STEPMOTHER PASIPHAË WAS WITH CHILD.
THE LABOR HAD BEEN LONG AND PAINFUL. HER SERVANT WOMEN WEREN'T SURE SHE WOULD SURVIVE.
BUT SHE DID AND SO DID HER CHILD. BUT NO ONE EXPECTED HIM TO LOOK LIKE—
—THIS!
MINOS REFUSED TO ADMIT THE CHILD WAS HIS.
IN FACT, HE WAS SO EMBARRASSED HE WOULD HAVE NOTHING TO DO WITH IT.
MINOS WENT TO THE TEMPLE TO FIND OUT WHAT TO DO WITH THE MONSTER.
HE RECEIVED MANY DIFFERENT SUGGESTIONS.
MOST SAID HE SHOULD DESTROY THE MONSTER. BUT HE COULDN'T DO THAT. HE KNEW THE GODS WOULD CURSE HIM IF HE KILLED HIS OWN CHILD.

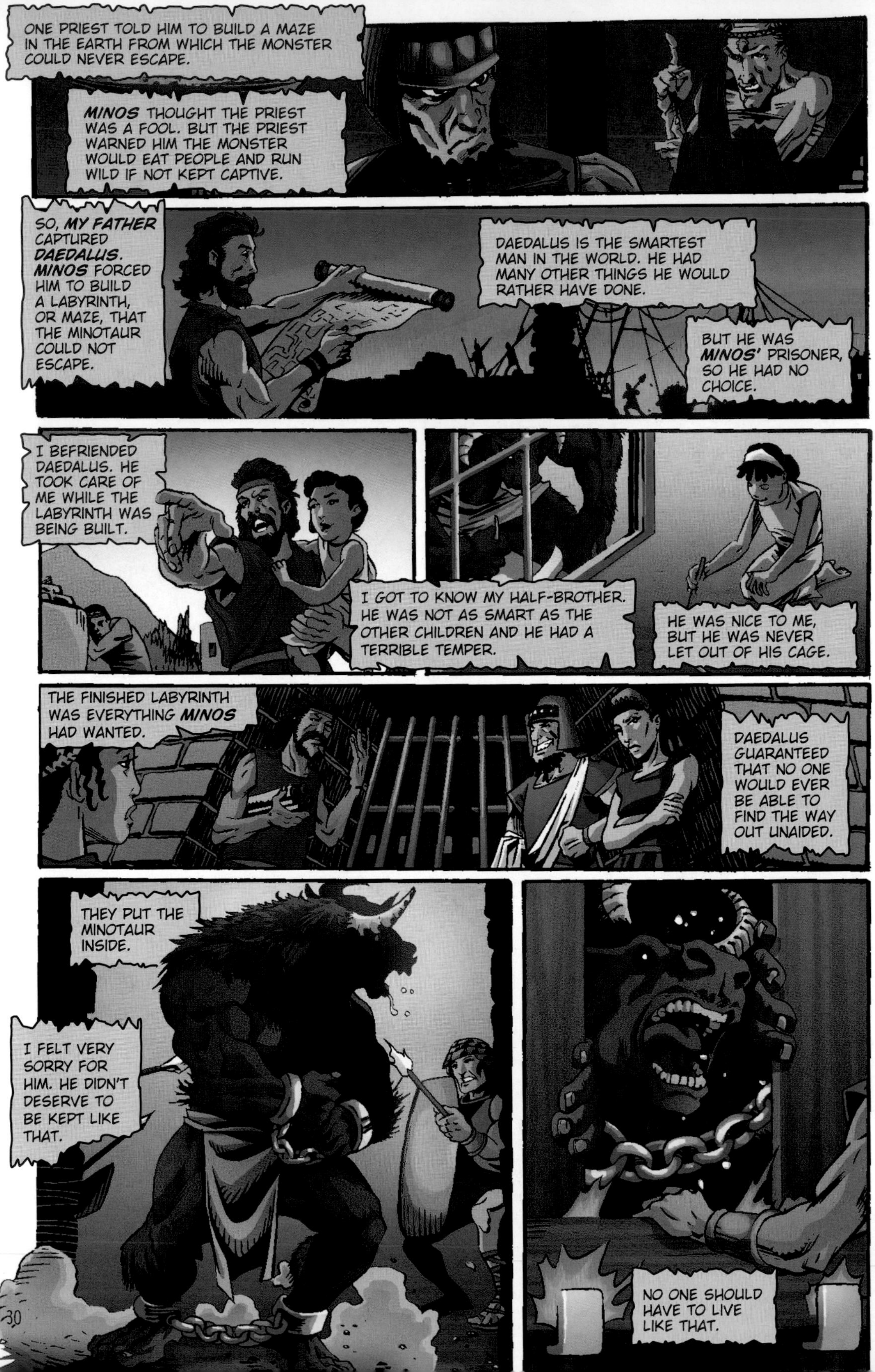
ONE PRIEST TOLD HIM TO BUILD A MAZE IN THE EARTH FROM WHICH THE MONSTER COULD NEVER ESCAPE.
MINOS THOUGHT THE PRIEST WAS A FOOL. BUT THE PRIEST WARNED HIM THE MONSTER WOULD EAT PEOPLE AND RUN WILD IF NOT KEPT CAPTIVE.
SO, MY FATHER CAPTURED DAEDALUS. MINOS FORCED HIM TO BUILD A LABYRINTH, OR MAZE, THAT THE MINOTAUR COULD NOT ESCAPE.
DAEDALUS IS THE SMARTEST MAN IN THE WORLD. HE HAD MANY OTHER THINGS HE WOULD RATHER HAVE DONE.
BUT HE WAS MINOS' PRISONER, SO HE HAD NO CHOICE.
I BEFRIENDED DAEDALUS. HE TOOK CARE OF ME WHILE THE LABYRINTH WAS BEING BUILT.
I GOT TO KNOW MY HALF-BROTHER. HE WAS NOT AS SMART AS THE OTHER CHILDREN AND HE HAD A TERRIBLE TEMPER.
HE WAS NICE TO ME, BUT HE WAS NEVER LET OUT OF HIS CAGE.
THE FINISHED LABYRINTH WAS EVERYTHING MINOS HAD WANTED.
DAEDALUS GUARANTEED THAT NO ONE WOULD EVER BE ABLE TO FIND THE WAY OUT UNAIDED.
THEY PUT THE MINOTAUR INSIDE.
I FELT VERY SORRY FOR HIM. HE DIDN'T DESERVE TO BE KEPT LIKE THAT.
NO ONE SHOULD HAVE TO LIVE LIKE THAT.

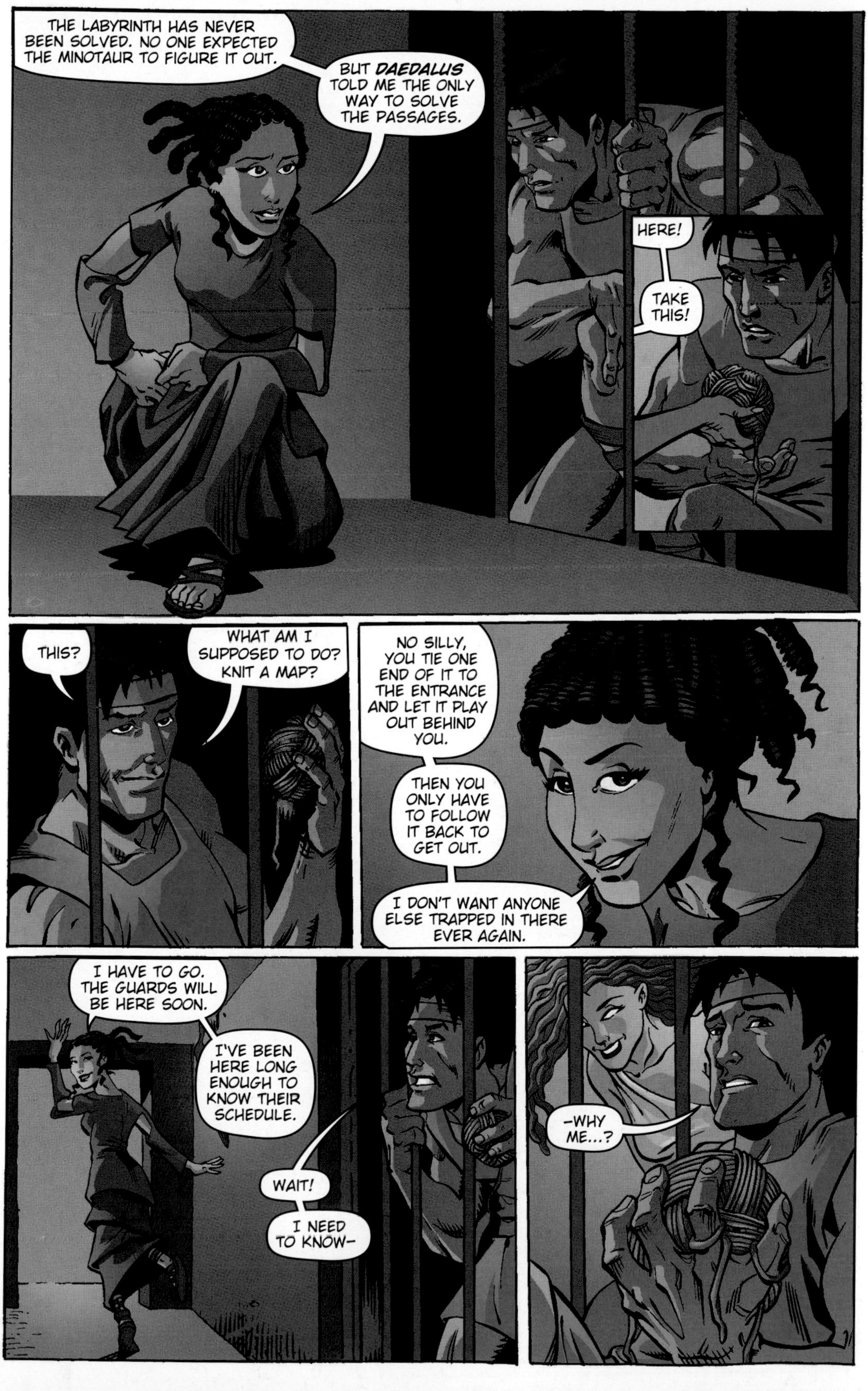
THE LABYRINTH HAS NEVER BEEN SOLVED. NO ONE EXPECTED THE MINOTAUR TO FIGURE IT OUT.
BUT DAEDALUS TOLD ME THE ONLY WAY TO SOLVE THE PASSAGES.
HERE!
TAKE THIS!
THIS?
WHAT AM I SUPPOSED TO DO? KNIT A MAP?
NO SILLY, YOU TIE ONE END OF IT TO THE ENTRANCE AND LET IT PLAY OUT BEHIND YOU.
THEN YOU ONLY HAVE TO FOLLOW IT BACK TO GET OUT.
I DON'T WANT ANYONE ELSE TRAPPED IN THERE EVER AGAIN.
I HAVE TO GO. THE GUARDS WILL BE HERE SOON.
I'VE BEEN HERE LONG ENOUGH TO KNOW THEIR SCHEDULE.
WAIT!
I NEED TO KNOW—
—WHY ME...?

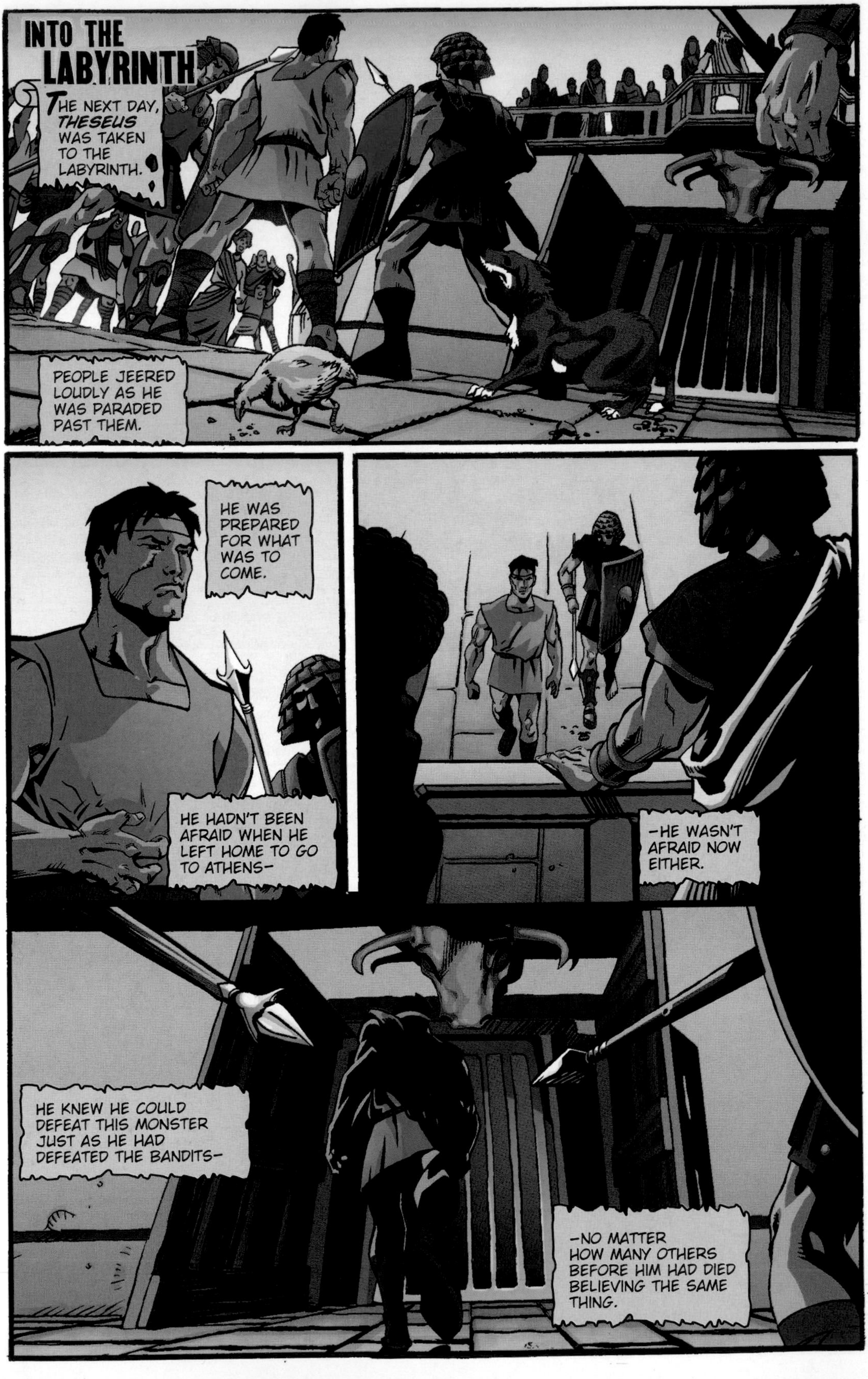
INTO THE LABYRINTH
THE NEXT DAY, THESEUS WAS TAKEN TO THE LABYRINTH.
PEOPLE JEERED LOUDLY AS HE WAS PARADED PAST THEM.
HE WAS PREPARED FOR WHAT WAS TO COME.
HE HADN'T BEEN AFRAID WHEN HE LEFT HOME TO GO TO ATHENS—
—HE WASN'T AFRAID NOW EITHER.
HE KNEW HE COULD DEFEAT THIS MONSTER JUST AS HE HAD DEFEATED THE BANDITS—
—NO MATTER HOW MANY OTHERS BEFORE HIM HAD DIED BELIEVING THE SAME THING.

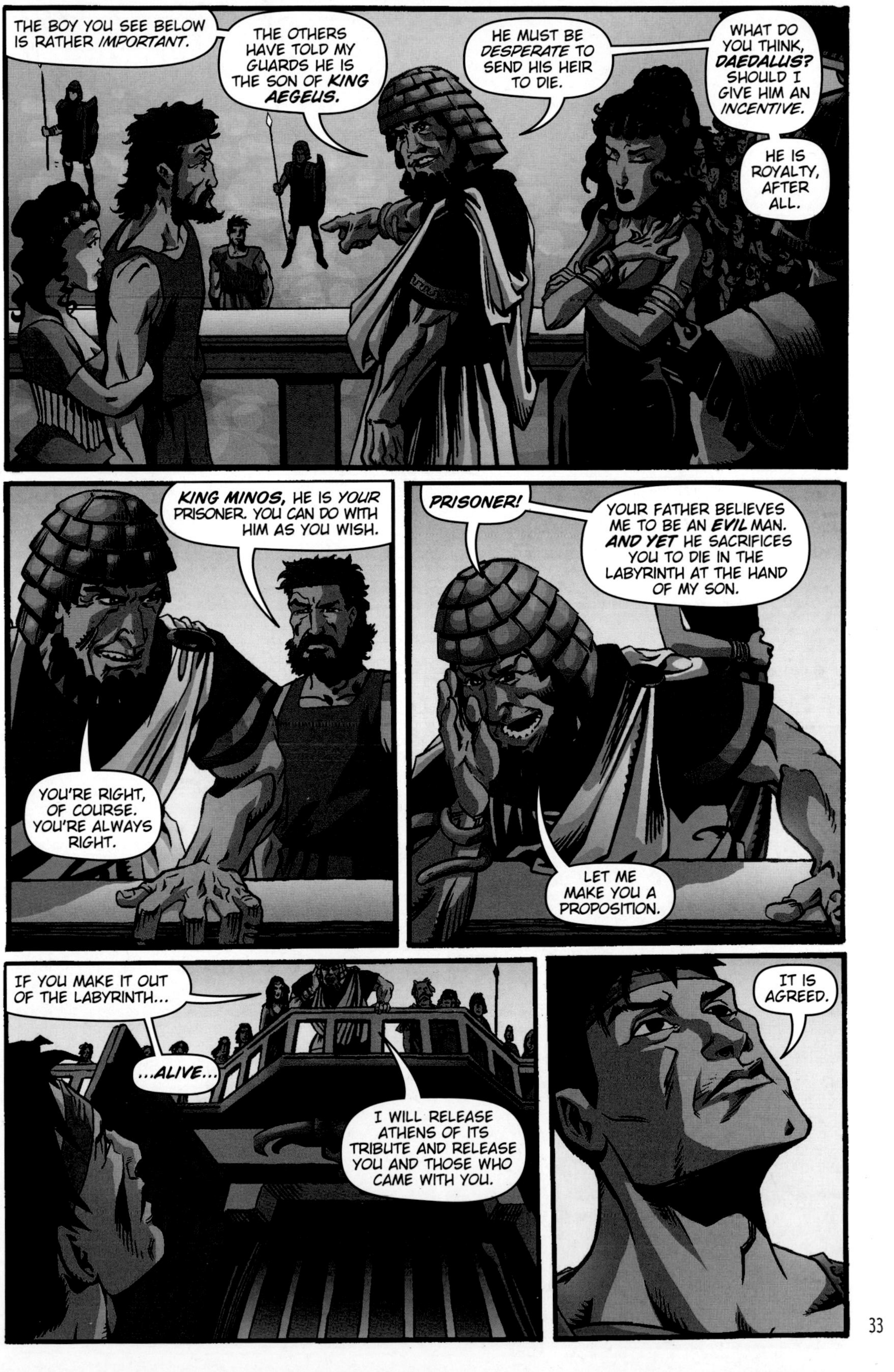
THE BOY YOU SEE BELOW IS RATHER *IMPORTANT*.
THE OTHERS HAVE TOLD MY GUARDS HE IS THE SON OF **KING AEGEUS.**
HE MUST BE *DESPERATE* TO SEND HIS HEIR TO DIE.
WHAT DO YOU THINK, **DAEDALUS?** SHOULD I GIVE HIM AN *INCENTIVE*.
HE IS ROYALTY, AFTER ALL.
***KING MINOS,*** HE IS *YOUR* PRISONER. YOU CAN DO WITH HIM AS YOU WISH.
YOU'RE RIGHT, OF COURSE. YOU'RE ALWAYS RIGHT.
***PRISONER!***
YOUR FATHER BELIEVES ME TO BE AN ***EVIL*** MAN. ***AND YET*** HE SACRIFICES YOU TO DIE IN THE LABYRINTH AT THE HAND OF MY SON.
LET ME MAKE YOU A PROPOSITION.
IF YOU MAKE IT OUT OF THE LABYRINTH...
...***ALIVE***...
I WILL RELEASE ATHENS OF ITS TRIBUTE AND RELEASE YOU AND THOSE WHO CAME WITH YOU.
IT IS AGREED.

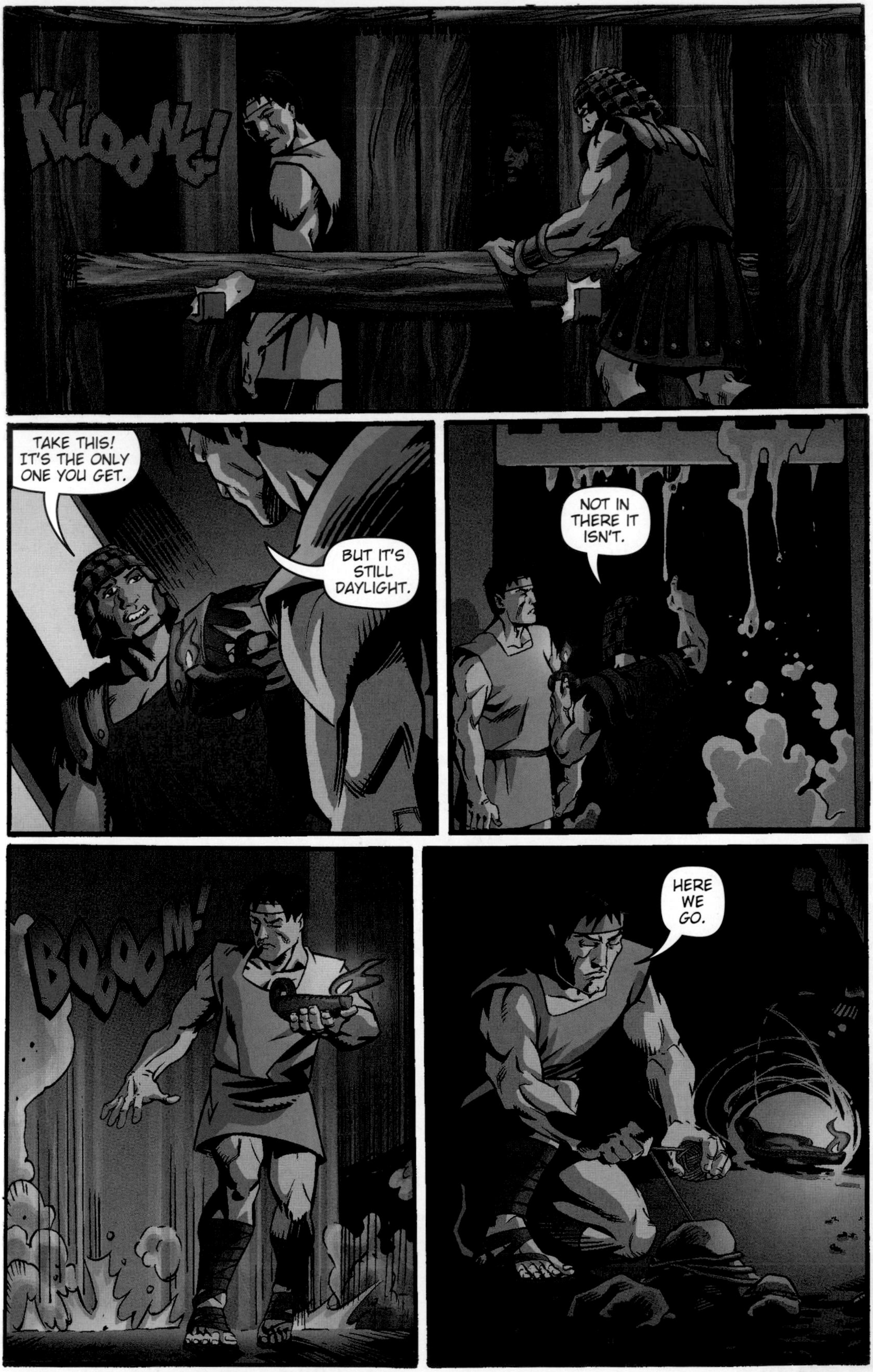
KLOONG!
TAKE THIS! IT'S THE ONLY ONE YOU GET.
BUT IT'S STILL DAYLIGHT.
NOT IN THERE IT ISN'T.
BOOOM!
HERE WE GO.

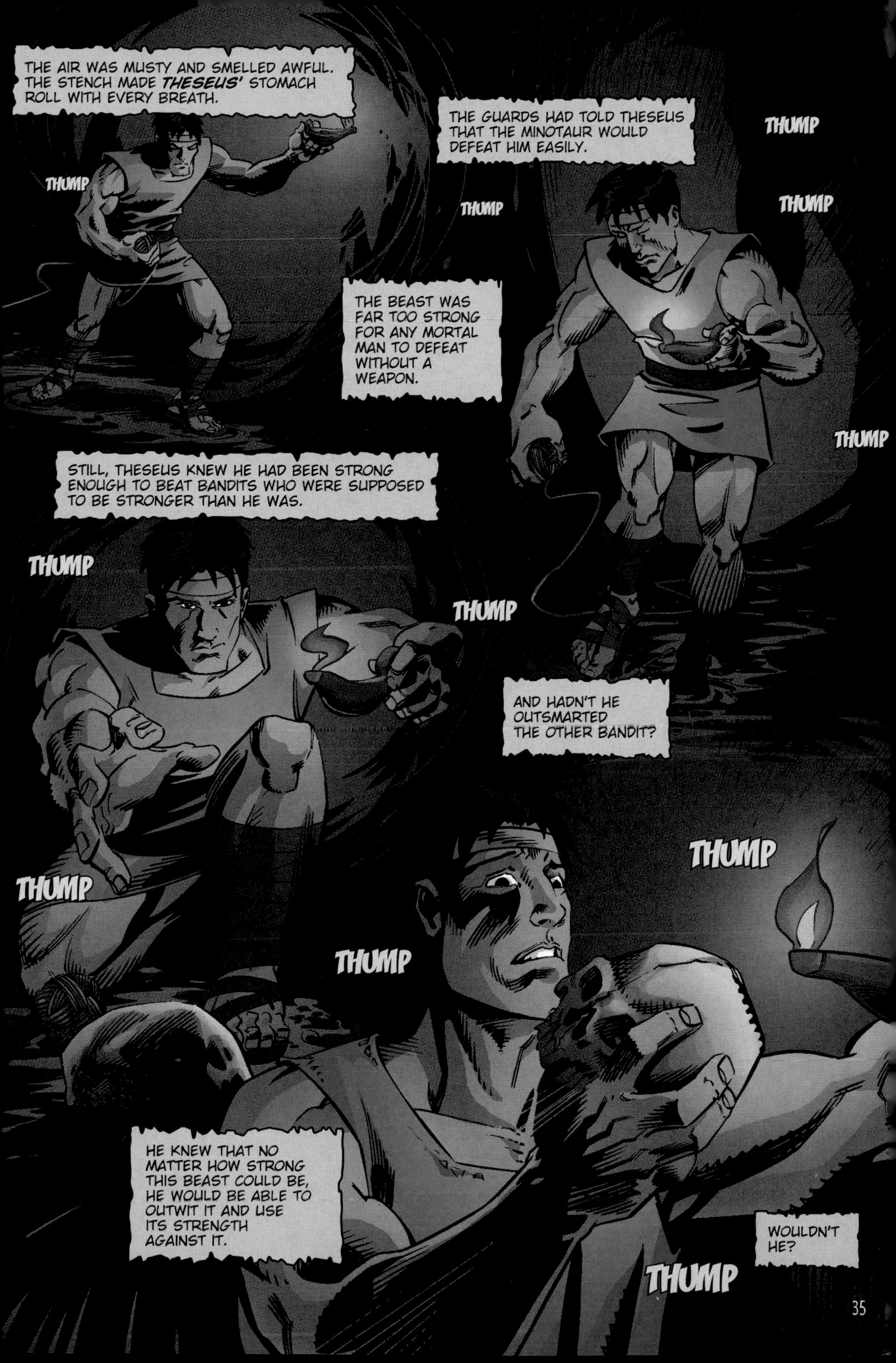

THE AIR WAS MUSTY AND SMELLED AWFUL. THE STENCH MADE *THESEUS'* STOMACH ROLL WITH EVERY BREATH.
THUMP
THE GUARDS HAD TOLD THESEUS THAT THE MINOTAUR WOULD DEFEAT HIM EASILY.
THUMP
THUMP
THUMP
THE BEAST WAS FAR TOO STRONG FOR ANY MORTAL MAN TO DEFEAT WITHOUT A WEAPON.
THUMP
STILL, THESEUS KNEW HE HAD BEEN STRONG ENOUGH TO BEAT BANDITS WHO WERE SUPPOSED TO BE STRONGER THAN HE WAS.
THUMP
THUMP
AND HADN'T HE OUTSMARTED THE OTHER BANDIT?
THUMP
THUMP
THUMP
HE KNEW THAT NO MATTER HOW STRONG THIS BEAST COULD BE, HE WOULD BE ABLE TO OUTWIT IT AND USE ITS STRENGTH AGAINST IT.
WOULDN'T HE?
THUMP

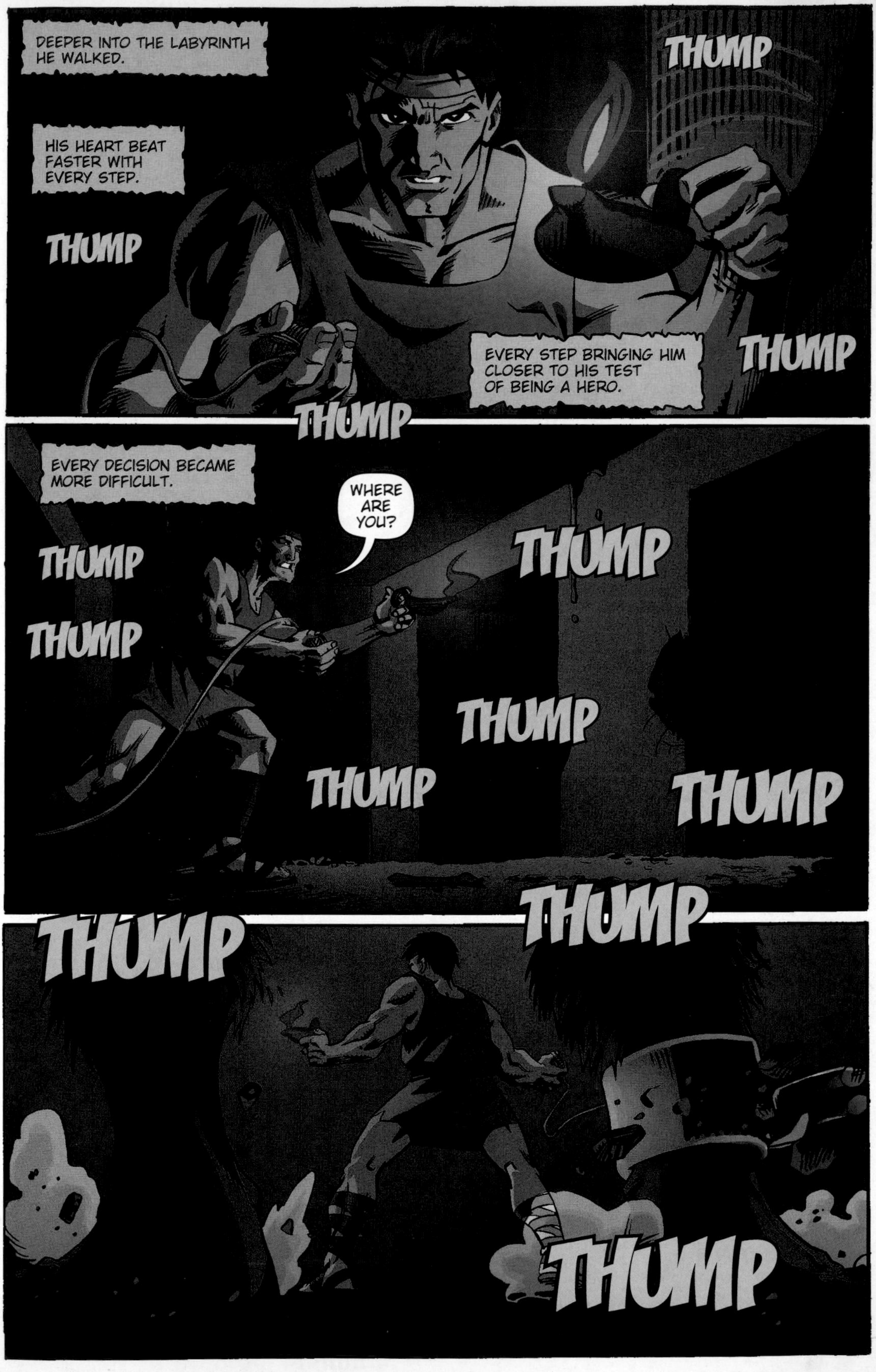
DEEPER INTO THE LABYRINTH HE WALKED.
THUMP
HIS HEART BEAT FASTER WITH EVERY STEP.
THUMP
EVERY STEP BRINGING HIM CLOSER TO HIS TEST OF BEING A HERO.
THUMP
THUMP
EVERY DECISION BECAME MORE DIFFICULT.
WHERE ARE YOU?
THUMP
THUMP
THUMP
THUMP
THUMP
THUMP
THUMP
THUMP
THUMP

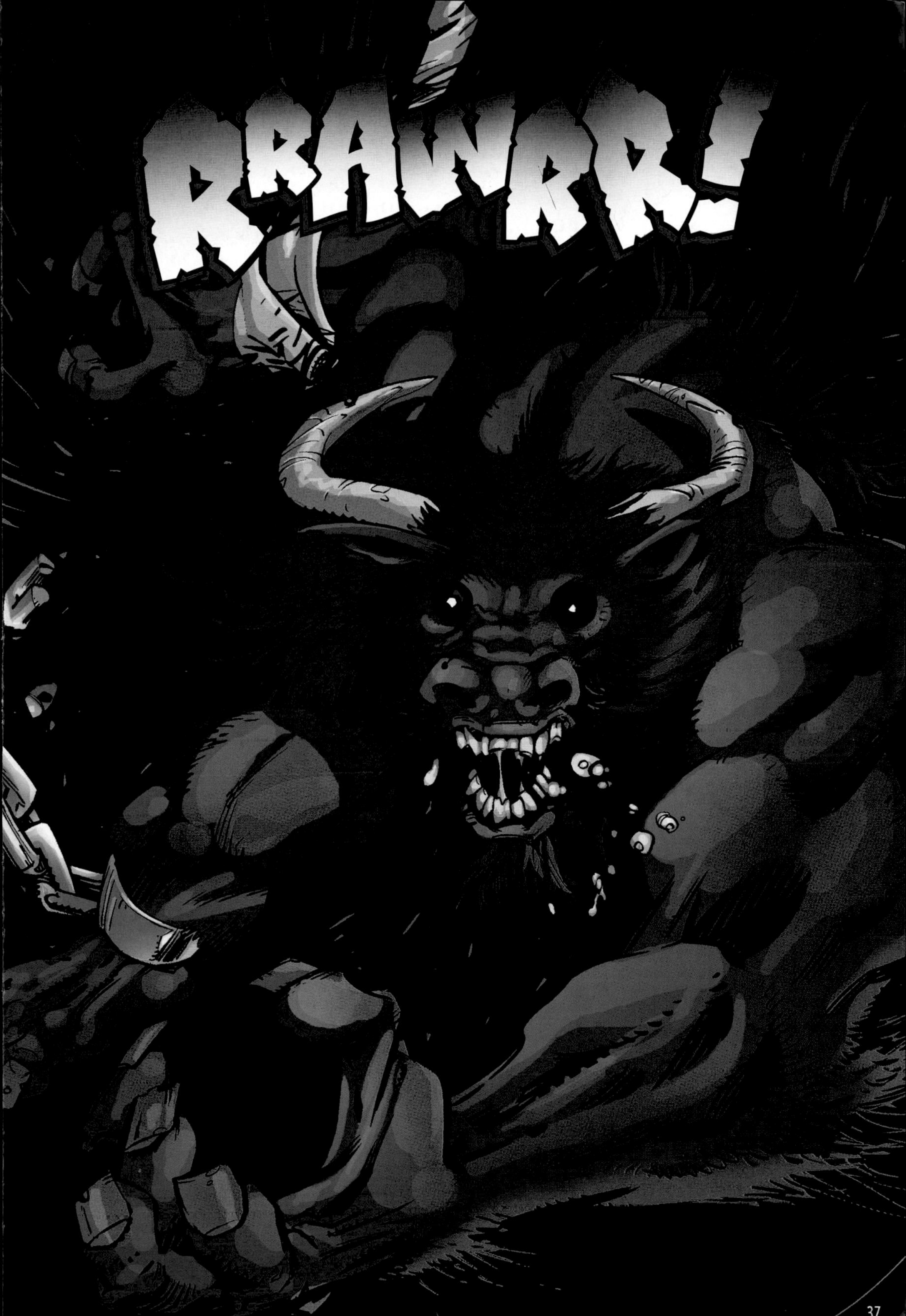
RRAWRR!

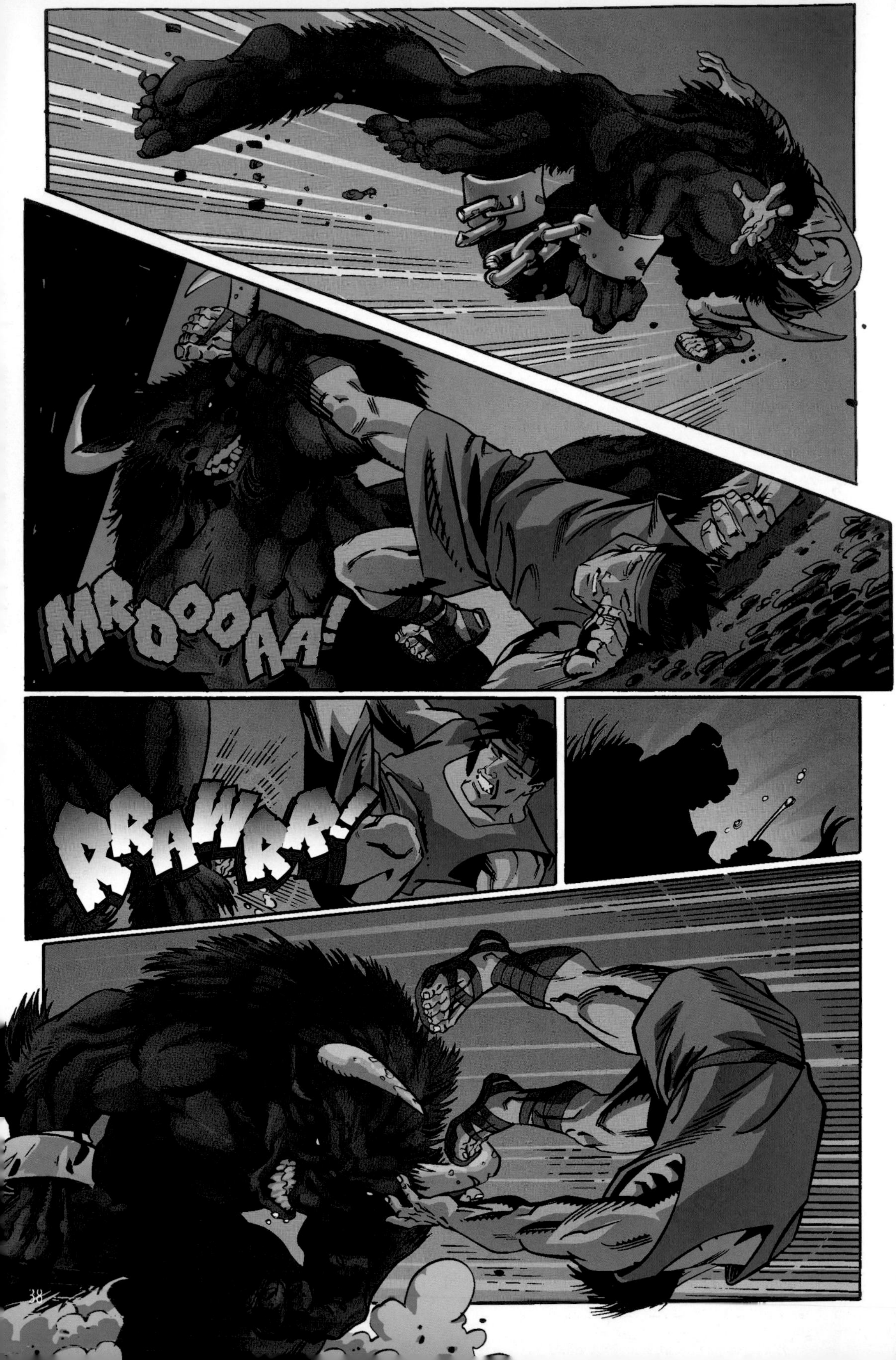
MROOOAA!
RRAWRR!

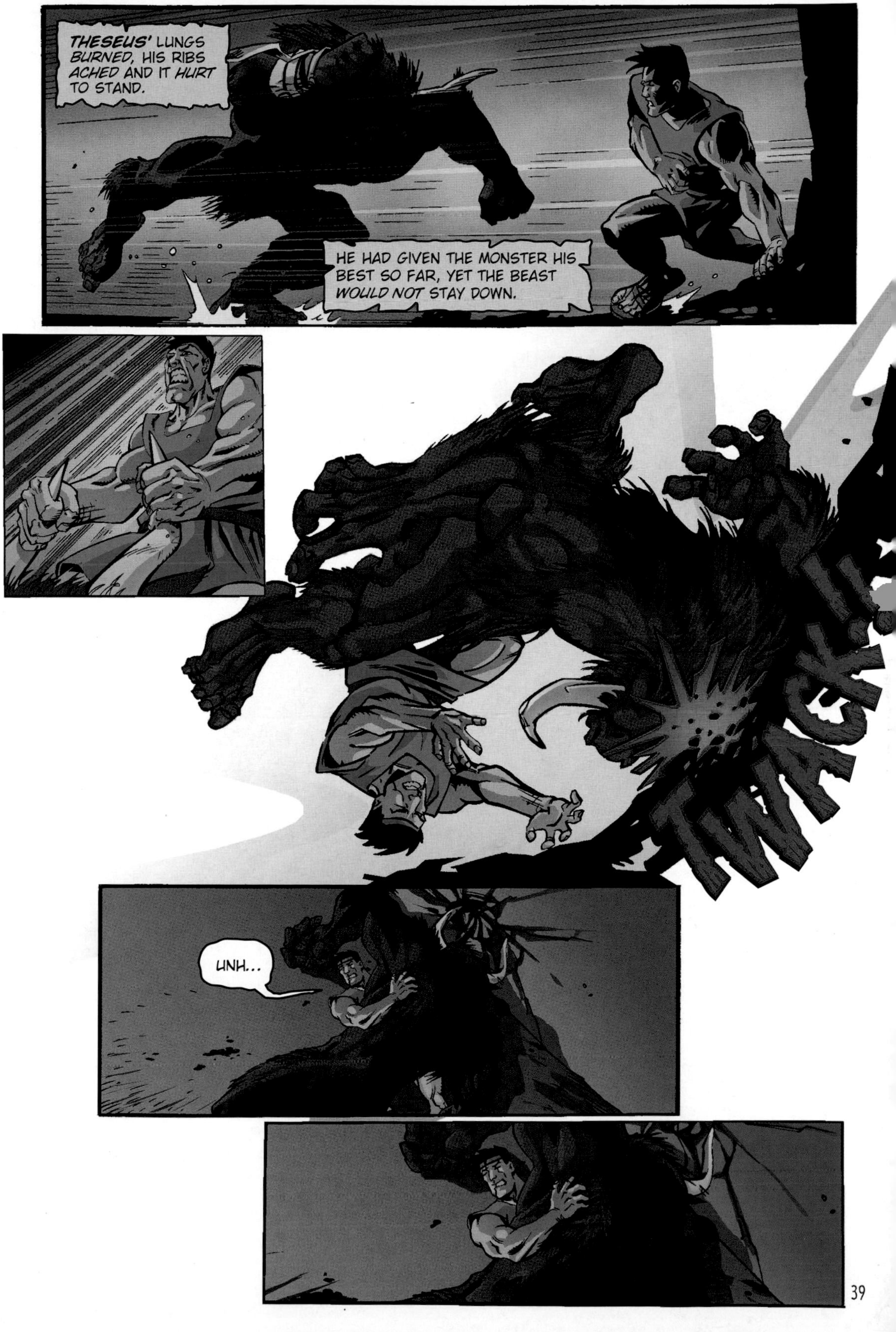

THESEUS' LUNGS BURNED, HIS RIBS ACHED AND IT HURT TO STAND.
HE HAD GIVEN THE MONSTER HIS BEST SO FAR, YET THE BEAST WOULD NOT STAY DOWN.
TWACK!!
UNH...

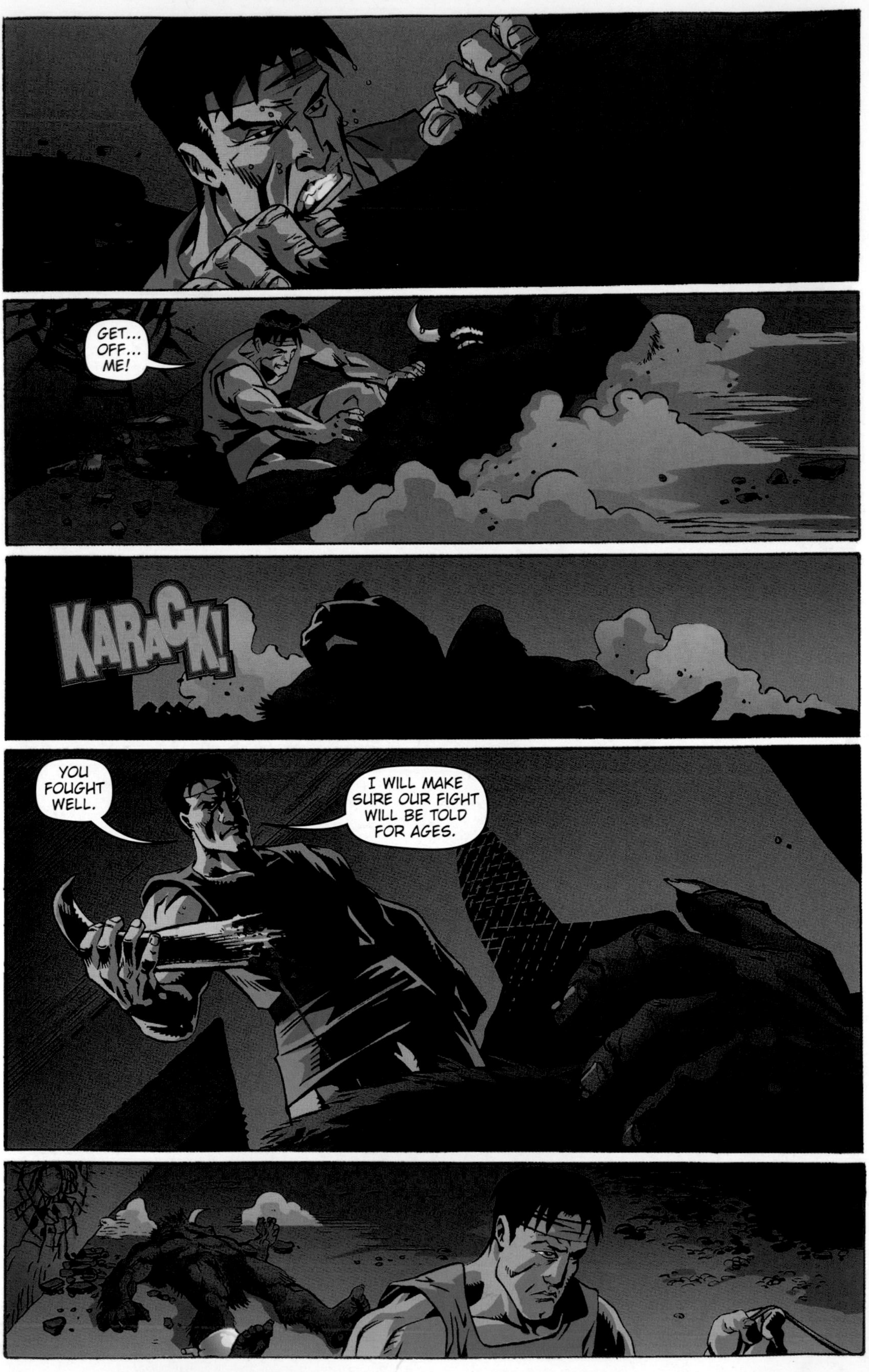
GET... OFF... ME!
KARACK!
YOU FOUGHT WELL.
I WILL MAKE SURE OUR FIGHT WILL BE TOLD FOR AGES.

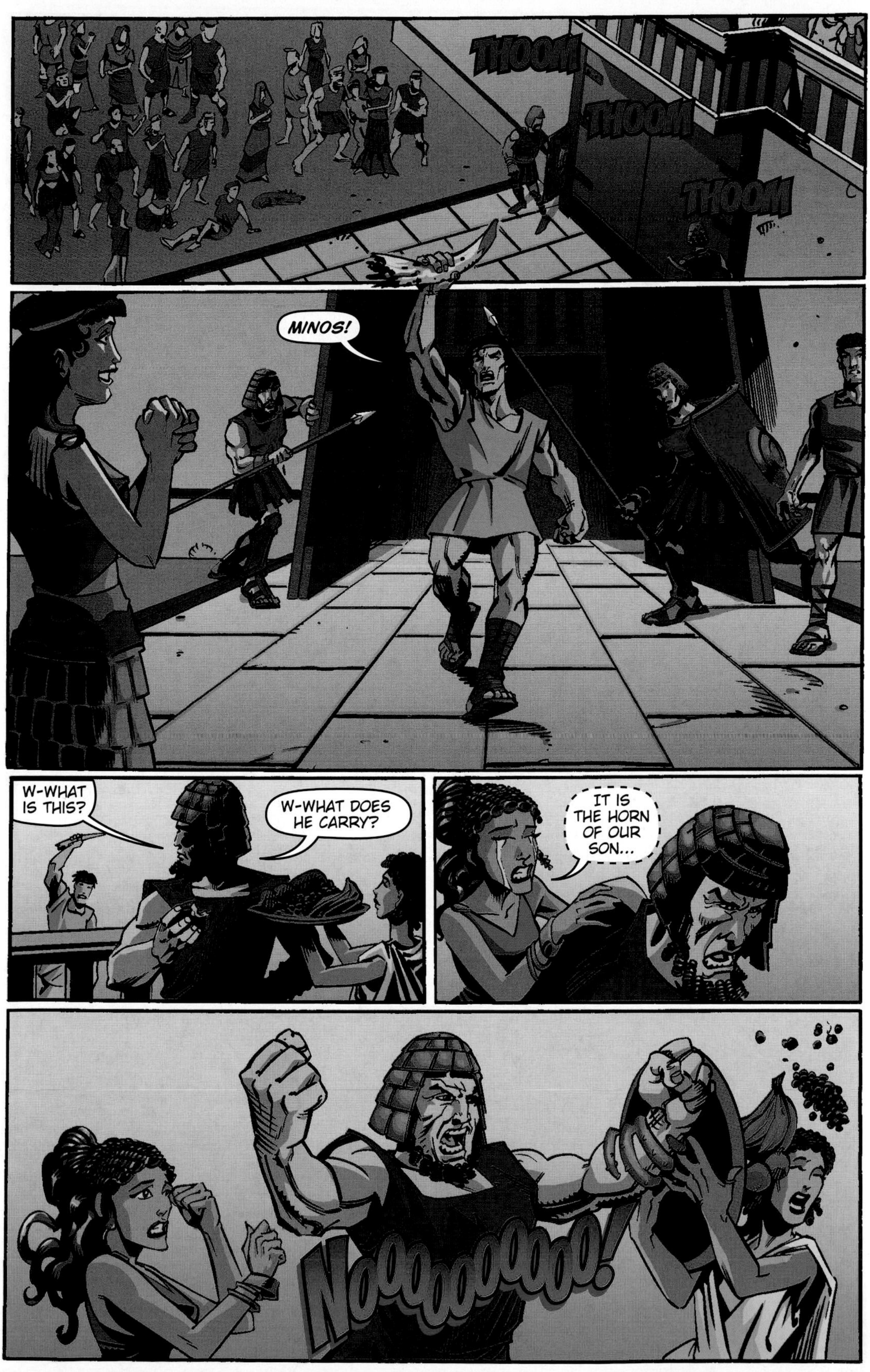
THOOM
THOOM
THOOM
MINOS!
W-WHAT IS THIS?
W-WHAT DOES HE CARRY?
IT IS THE HORN OF OUR SON...
NOOOOOOOOO!

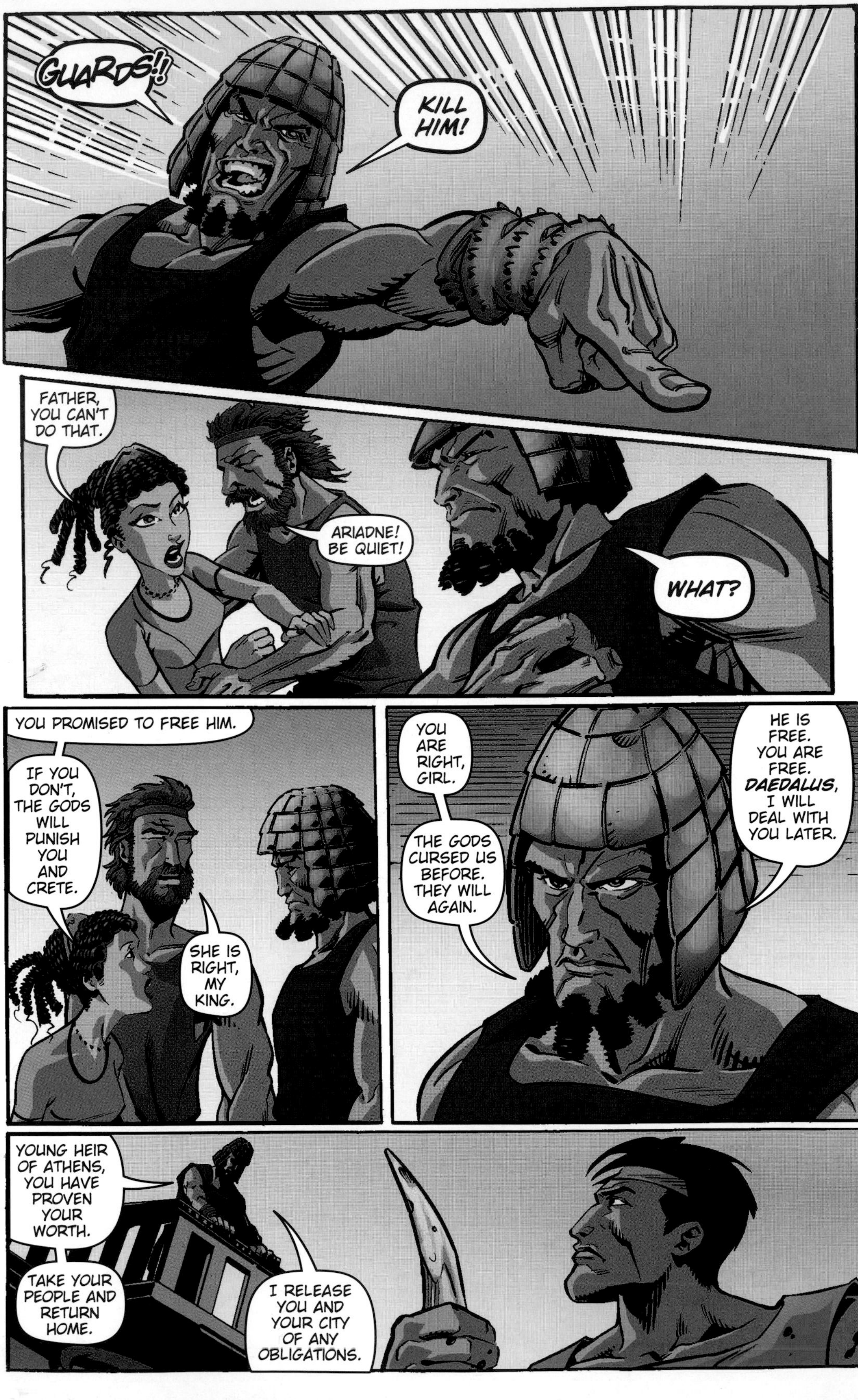
GUARDS!!
KILL HIM!
FATHER, YOU CAN'T DO THAT.
ARIADNE! BE QUIET!
WHAT?
YOU PROMISED TO FREE HIM.
IF YOU DON'T, THE GODS WILL PUNISH YOU AND CRETE.
SHE IS RIGHT, MY KING.
YOU ARE RIGHT, GIRL.
THE GODS CURSED US BEFORE. THEY WILL AGAIN.
HE IS FREE. YOU ARE FREE. DAEDALUS, I WILL DEAL WITH YOU LATER.
YOUNG HEIR OF ATHENS, YOU HAVE PROVEN YOUR WORTH.
TAKE YOUR PEOPLE AND RETURN HOME.
I RELEASE YOU AND YOUR CITY OF ANY OBLIGATIONS.

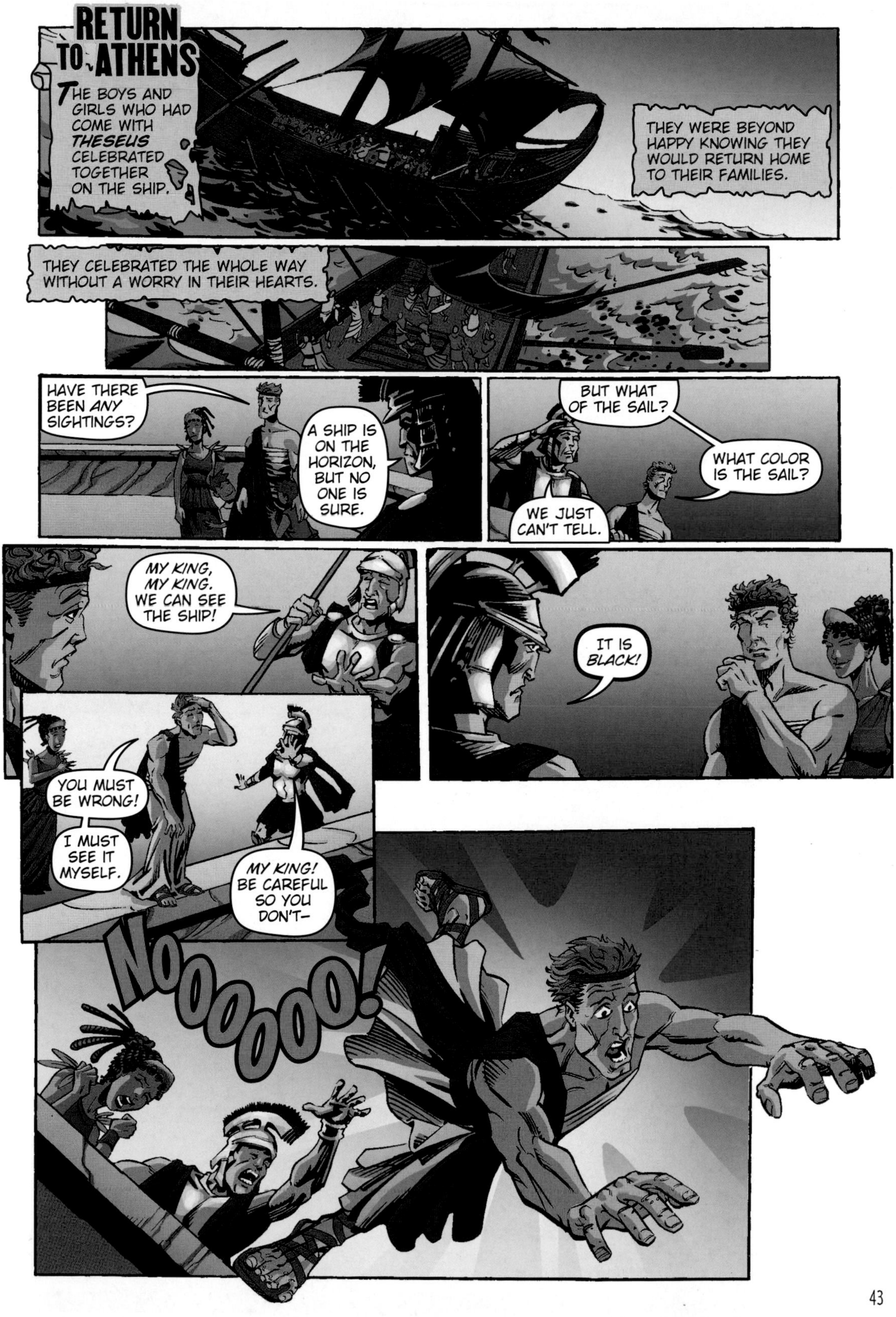
RETURN TO ATHENS
THE BOYS AND GIRLS WHO HAD COME WITH THESEUS CELEBRATED TOGETHER ON THE SHIP.
THEY WERE BEYOND HAPPY KNOWING THEY WOULD RETURN HOME TO THEIR FAMILIES.
THEY CELEBRATED THE WHOLE WAY WITHOUT A WORRY IN THEIR HEARTS.
HAVE THERE BEEN ANY SIGHTINGS?
A SHIP IS ON THE HORIZON, BUT NO ONE IS SURE.
BUT WHAT OF THE SAIL?
WHAT COLOR IS THE SAIL?
WE JUST CAN'T TELL.
MY KING, MY KING. WE CAN SEE THE SHIP!
IT IS BLACK!
YOU MUST BE WRONG!
I MUST SEE IT MYSELF.
MY KING! BE CAREFUL SO YOU DON'T—
NOOOOOO!

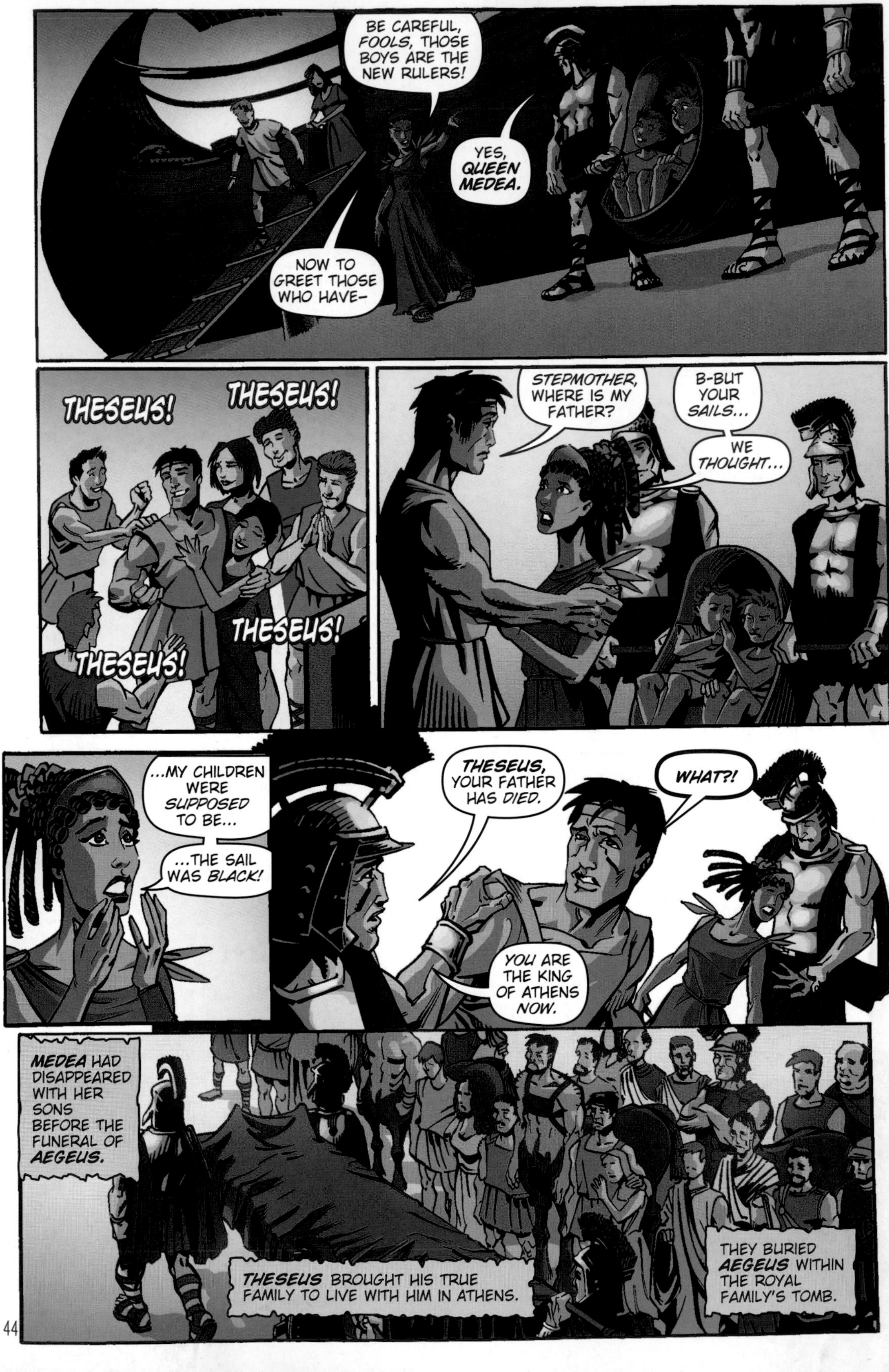
BE CAREFUL, FOOLS, THOSE BOYS ARE THE NEW RULERS!
YES, QUEEN MEDEA.
NOW TO GREET THOSE WHO HAVE-
THESEUS!
THESEUS!
THESEUS!
THESEUS!
STEPMOTHER, WHERE IS MY FATHER?
B-BUT YOUR SAILS...
WE THOUGHT...
...MY CHILDREN WERE SUPPOSED TO BE...
...THE SAIL WAS BLACK!
THESEUS, YOUR FATHER HAS DIED.
WHAT?!
YOU ARE THE KING OF ATHENS NOW.
MEDEA HAD DISAPPEARED WITH HER SONS BEFORE THE FUNERAL OF AEGEUS.
THESEUS BROUGHT HIS TRUE FAMILY TO LIVE WITH HIM IN ATHENS.
THEY BURIED AEGEUS WITHIN THE ROYAL FAMILY'S TOMB.

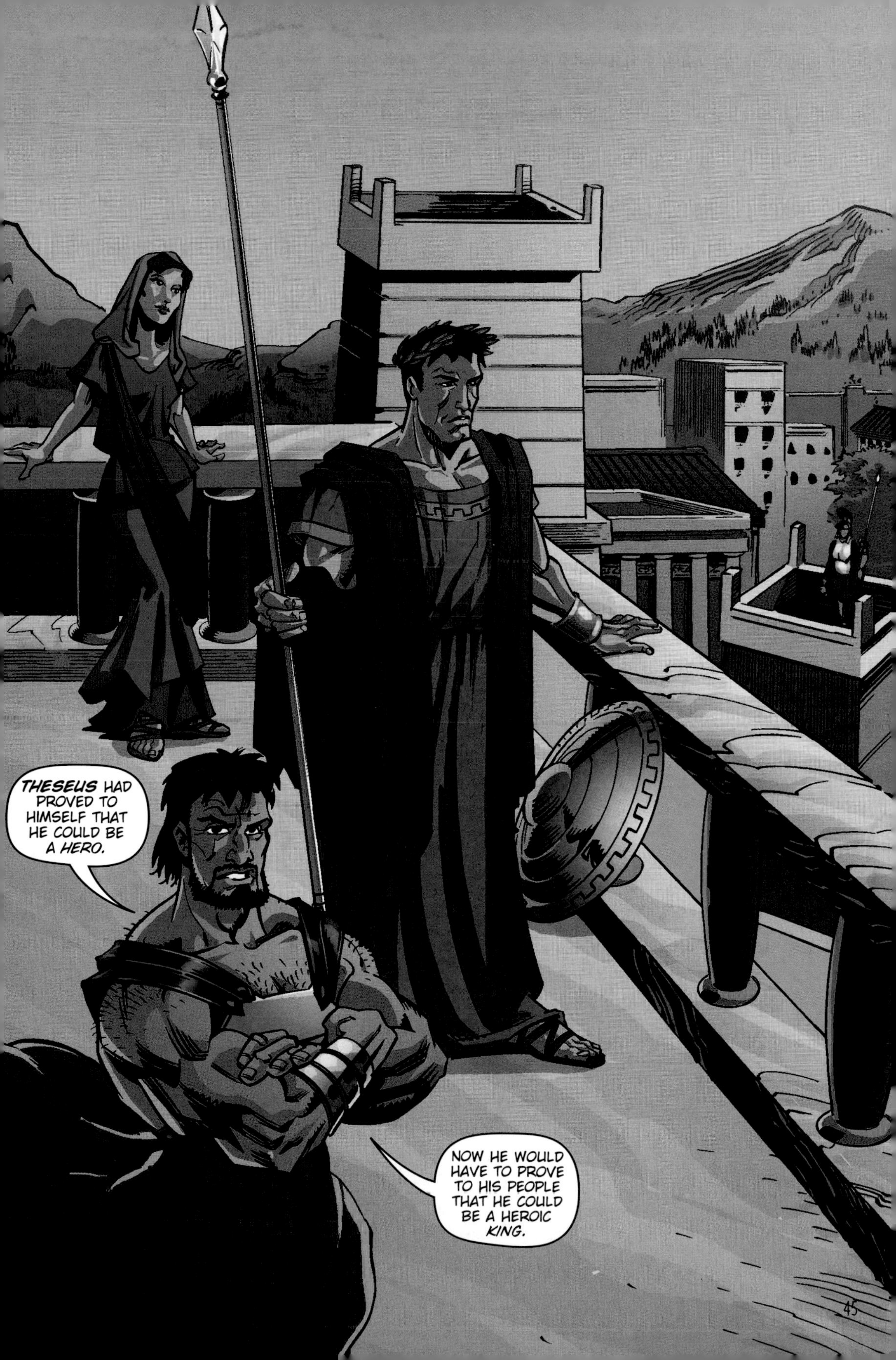
THESEUS HAD PROVED TO HIMSELF THAT HE COULD BE A HERO.
NOW HE WOULD HAVE TO PROVE TO HIS PEOPLE THAT HE COULD BE A HEROIC KING.

# GLOSSARY AND PRONUNCIATION GUIDE

**AEGEUS** (eh-*jee*-us): the king of Athens and Theseus' father

**AETHRA** (*ee*-thrah): Aegeus' wife and Theseus' mother

**APHRODITE** (a-fruh-*dy*-tee): the Greek goddess of love and beauty

**ARIADNE** (ah-ree-*ad*-nee): Minos' daughter, who helps Theseus to escape the labyrinth

**ATHENS** (*a*-thenz): one of the great historic Greek city states

**CONNIDUS** (kun-*eye*-duhs): Theseus' centaur (half-horse, half-human) tutor

**CRETE** (kreet): a large island in the eastern Mediterranean Sea, off the southern coast of Greece

**DAEDALUS** (*deh*-deh-lus): the engineering genius who built the labyrinth for King Minos

**HERAKLES** (*hair*-uh-kleez): a legendary Greek hero; also known by his Roman name, Hercules

**LABYRINTH** (*la*-buh-rinth): a place full of confusing passageways and dead ends; a maze

**MEDEA** (muh-*dee*-uh): Aegeus' wife

**MINOS** (*my*-nohs): the king of Crete and the father of the Minotaur and of Ariadne

**MINOTAUR** (*my*-nuh-tor): a ferocious half-man, half-bull; the son of Minos and Pasiphaë

**PASIPHAË** (pas-uh-*fay*): wife of Minos, mother of the Minotaur

**PERIPHETES** (puh-reh-*fee*-teez): a bandit who preys on travelers along the road to Athens

**PITTHEUS** (pit-*thee*-us): Theseus' grandfather

**POSEIDON** (poh-*sy*-duhn): the Greek god of the sea

**PROCRUSTES** (proh-*krus*-teez): an evil innkeeper who murders his guests by stretching them or cutting off their limbs

**SINIS** (*sin*-uhs): a sinister bandit who kills his victims by forcing them to hold the tops of two trees at the same time, causing them to be torn apart

**THESEUS** (*thee*-see-uhs): son of Aegeus and Aethra; Aegeus' successor as king of Athens

# FURTHER READING, WEBSITES, AND MOVIES


Bolton, Lesley. *The Everything Classical Mythology Book: Greek and Roman Gods, Goddesses, Heroes, and Monsters from Ares to Zeus.* Avon, MA: Adams Media Corporation, 2002. This who's who guide introduces young readers to Greek and Roman mythology.

Day, Nancy. *Your Travel Guide to Ancient Greece.* Minneapolis: Twenty-First Century Books, 2001. Day prepares readers for a trip back to ancient Greece, including which cities to visit, how to get around, what to wear, and how to fit in with the locals.

*Jim Henson's The Storyteller: Greek Myths.* DVD. Directed by David Garfath and John Madden. Hollywood, CA: Sony Pictures, 2004. In this entertaining series of stories, four famous Greek myths—including Theseus and the Minotaur—are brought to life using live actors and puppets.

Limke, Jeff. *Jason: Quest for the Golden Fleece.* Minneapolis: Graphic Universe, 2007. Read about the exciting adventures of another great Greek hero, Jason, and his relationship with a certain woman named Medea.

*MythWeb.* http://www.mythweb.com/index.html. This site, with a searchable encyclopedia, provides students with information on gods, goddesses, and places in Greek myth, as well as ample information about Theseus.

Storrie, Paul D. *Hercules: The Twelve Labors.* Minneapolis: Graphic Universe, 2007. Learn about Theseus' hero and inspiration, Hercules, one of Greece's greatest legends.


# CREATING *THESEUS: BATTLING THE MINOTAUR*

To craft this tale for the Graphic Myths and Legends series, author Jeff Limke consulted two of the most famous anthologies of Greek myths, Edith Hamilton's *Mythology* and *Bulfinch's Mythology* by Thomas Bulfinch. Artist John McCrea referenced numerous historical and traditional sources to give the art and authentic look, from classical Greek architecture to the clothing, weapons, and armor worn by the characters. Professor David Mulroy ensured historical and visual accuracy.

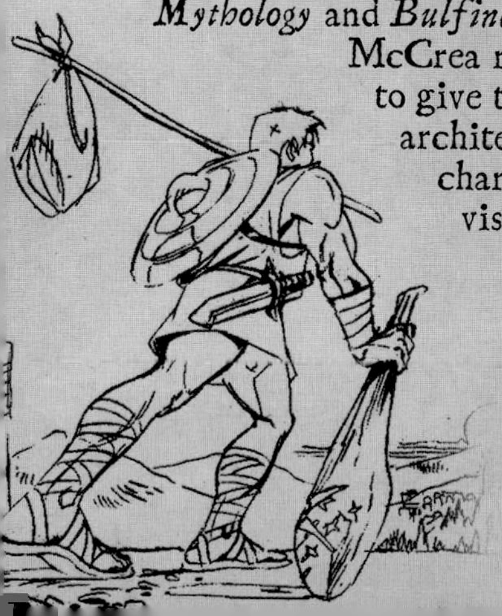

*original pencil from page 15*

# INDEX

# ABOUT THE AUTHOR AND THE ARTIST

**JEFF LIMKE** was raised in North Dakota. There he read, listened to, and marveled at stories from the day he learned to read. He later taught stories for many years and has written adaptations of them. Some of his stories have been published by Arrow Comics, Caliber Comics, and Kenzer and Company. His titles for Graphic Universe include *King Arthur: Excalibur Unsheathed*; *Isis & Osiris: To the Ends of the Earth*; *Thor & Loki: In the Land of Giants*; *Jason: The Quest for the Golden Fleece*; and *Arthur & Lancelot: The Fight for Camelot*. Along the way, he got married, and he and his wife had a daughter who loves to read, listen to, and marvel at stories.

**JOHN McCREA** was born in Belfast, Northern Ireland. He has been drawing comics professionally for nearly twenty years. His work has become well known through comics for both DC and Marvel, including titles for such series as *Judge Dredd*, *Hitman*, and *Section 8*. He currently lives in Birmingham, England.